US BUSINESS OUTSOURING STRATEGY ADVANTAGES

JOHN LOK

Contents

Foreword

The strategic implementation of outsourcing within the United States economy is a multifaceted process that, when executed correctly, serves as a catalyst for business development by allowing firms to focus on core competencies while leveraging external specialized expertise. In my analysis of outsourcing strategies, emphasizes that the primary objective for U.S. businesses is not merely cost reduction, but the optimization of value chains to achieve sustainable competitive advantages.

Preface

This book divides two parts. It explains how US organizations implement outsourcing may bring advantage. This book first part indicates nowadays, outsourcing is popular strategy to any global organizations. But businessmen neglect outsourcing strategy has disadvantages to influence global macro economy wealth inequality.This book explains why outsourcing strategy can bring what advantages to consumer market, but it can also bring disadvantages to influence global economy inequality. I shall indicate evidences to explain why US organizations choose outsoucing stragegy can bring benefits to themselves, but they will influence global macro economy wealth inequality. Why US business envirnment outsourcing strategy is one main factor influence global wealth inequality.

This book seond part concerns to give evidences to explain whether the wealth inequality occuence is influenced by the super rich country, America. Finally, I shall explain why I think America outsoucing strategy can influence to wealth inequality in the world really. This book is suitable to any students who like to research US outsoucing strategy is one main factor to influence global wealth inequality.

Prologue

Table of contents

CHAPTER ONE

Outsourcing brings US organizations advantages and disadvantages

Information technology outsourcing

Can US outsoucing information technology strategy influence other countries 's information technology development to be raised? To answer this question, we need to know why organization needs to outsource thier computer department duties to other IT organizations to work.

In any organization information technology department, information system operations remain the predominant function outsourced, other functions are also being performed by external service providers and the relationship is between outsourcing and certain demographics: size, industry is formation intensity. The results suggest that system operations remain being performed by external service providers. Further, industry and information intensity has some influence on the extent of outsourcing of certain functions.

The first reason is cost reduction, trying to remain competitive and up-to-date is becoming a financial burden to many organizations. This is true particularly in fields, such as banking and financial services, health care and manufacturing. Hiring outsiders to handle part or even all of its information system often helps an organization to provide better services and maintain a competitive advantage. The information technology industry choice of outsourcing factor is related to size, industry type and information technology.

The second reason is technological and/or human resources in the management of the information technology infrastructure skill improvement. The information technology department outsourcing service to external service provider, includes the degree of internalization of technological resources and the degree of internalization of human resources. Some economists defined internalization of outsourcing service is as ownership is by the focal organization which takes on full control with profit and loss responsibility. Also who define outsourcing is as involving a significant use of resources, either technological and/or human resources, external to the organizational hierarchy in the management of the information technology infrastructure. So the information technology external service providers includes: applications development and maintenance, systems operations, networks/telecommunications management and user computing support, system planning and management purchase of application software, but excludes business consulting services, after-sale vendor services and the lease of telephone lines etc. outsourcing services.

The third reason is economics of scale in areas of hardware, software. This pressure is seen as the most significant factor driving today's corporate interest. An outsourcing service provision might be in a position to exploit economics of scale in areas of hardware, software and staff since it pools different kind of technological projects from many service receivers. Outsourcing information technological service can reduce the corporate's cost with the high level of IT investment, there are increasing pressures to move away from fixed expenditure, corporate overhead towards a more direct variable cost approach to control the IT operations. The IT costs can become predictable for overruns is often placed on the service provider. Outsourcing service can allow the service to gain immediate access to competitiveness in delivering products or services as well as to avoid of obsolescence risk, due to the changes in the nature of the IT infrastructure, the risk of obsolescence is high. Outsourcing can allow the service provider has the ability to diversify these risks across a broad range of service receivers. However, long term contracts might in spread the risk, the weakness is back to the receiver.

It seems outsourcing IT service has also these disadvantages: such as, loss of flexibility or managerial control. Outsourcing reduces real or perceived control over both quality real or perceived control over both the quality of software and the timetable of project since the work is now being carried out by people not under direct supervision. It also threats to long term career prospects to information system professionals because many of them do not find suitable. Is jobs or promising career paths in both areas of the corporation. Outsourcing also increases coordination cost. It may requires increasing time to communicate and coordinate with the service provider. Traditionally, the formal meeting cost of negotiating and monitoring the outsourcing contract are potentially wide ranging, indirect and substantial increasing, such as, additional releasing or transferring employees, in license transfer by software vendors and in re-negotiating contracts costs. So, the IT industry of profit motivates service provider might not be in the least interests of the outsourcing service receivers. Some IT service providers are in the business of maximizing their profit at any cost, this could run counter to a service receiver's interest.

Outsourcing or in-sourcing in human resource supply chain factor

Can US HR outsouring influence other countries HR agency organizations earn income? To choosing of outsourcing or insourcing in human resource supply chain factor of the controlling service demanders needs to concern this issues: Should human resource activities be provided in house or should all or past of those activities be outsourced? The relationship between organizational structure and the HR function is an important variable. The individual activities that comprise HR systems include not only the employee life cycle from recruiting to termination, but also planning for organizational staffing needs and improving organizational effectiveness. How organizations need to outsource HR function to not care employees knowledge and skill is a factor to influence any organizations choose to outsourcing non core employees when which have no any right employees to be promoted to do the position. For example, firms engage in HR outsourcing to reduce management access HR expertise, achieve workforce flexibility, focus managerial resources and keep up with changing workplace negotiations. Also, supporting the tend is the availability of common technology platform, which can reduce costs for organizations and risks. However, organizations are afraid of losing some control over delivery of outsourcing services and finding themselves dependent on the vendor or liable for the vendors actions where there are both benefits and challenges may be informed by the structure of the relationship between client firms and these organizations offering the outsourced activities to client firms.

What variables are impacted by HR outsourcing of staffing? Which include: administrative costs for labor expense, client firm to HR relations, HR regulatory competency requirement, knowledge of cost factors, e.g. billing and pay rates, vendor markups and margins, vendor management competency requirement, client and vendor relationship, communication is between client managers and staffing vendor, employee data-available, data quality control, data security, match with job requirement, employee quality, inter-vendor competition, mining of client talent by vendor , quality content for preferred staffing vendor, standardization of business process (intra-company), strategic focus of client firm, demands on client managers vendor competency and external economic environmental viability.

However, it has dynamic relationship between the client firms and staffing vendors. Moreover, the models of human resource supply chain, every has different set of advantages and disadvantages for the client firms. The models can be relate to the decision making process on outsourcing of human resources. As strategic services tactic decisions have an important impact or selecting the particular HR outsourcing model that a client firm adopter. The another model is the balance of power and control over managing the control workers differ to decide what every worker individual skills or abilities outsourcing demand. Moreover, local contracting is also the predominant traditional model for outsourcing staffing with non-core employees. A client firm usually uses several staffing vendors to meet temporary staffing needs for seasonal functions, employee absences and special projects. The advantages of local contracting are high touch and high quality of service by staffing vendors, minimal bureaucracy, empowerment of hiring any high qualified employees to get the job done, and a relatively better fit between specific staffing vendors and functional needs.

The disadvantages of local contracting can increase costs from non-standardization of hiring practices and procedures across the client form, a significant amount of word of mouth and subjective quality issues, high local costs and client firm us subjected to the capabilities of the staffing vendors and contract employees. However, local HR contracting is the most flexible, high quality, but expense, inefficient and ineffective HR outsourcing model for the client firm. Another model is the working period to be decided to outsource HR contracting. In this situation, in the short term and on a day-to-day basis, the client firm aims to achieve on economy of scale with its staffing vendors. The total costs of temporary workers as well as internal costs for contracting with several different vendors are higher than if it needs one staffing vendors to meet all its needs. So, the client company can set the reasonable pricing that it pays for its temporary outsourcing staffs. Each staffing vendor secures a different rate range with each vendor as opposed as one contact. In the long term, it is benefiting, each specialized staffing vendor is able to fully work with each function needs temporary utilization is better than the average. Mismatches are fewer. Functional departments are able to receive a high quality / high touch service in any time period. Another model is the centralizing is when the department standardizes the staffing process to drive costs down of temporary workers. This tends to occur when a percentage of non-core employees reach a certain ratio of core employees. The advantages include more uniform standards in hiring process, billing rates and pay rates, departmental hiring managers can refocus their effort to choose outsourcing staffing, criteria may be established for a performed suppliers list and greater security for the staffing established vendors that offer higher quality services. The disadvantages include new departmental responsibilities in HR which decreases outsourcing efficiencies for the organizations daily administrative direction is rather than long term strategic direction. Usually lacking qualifications to fulfill the responsibilities, overall, centralizing of HR outsourcing is that firms can achieve more standardization which additional bureaucratic costs and the necessary non-core jobs do not get done as a need. Another model is purchasing HR, which manages staffing vendors from HR to the purchasing unit of an organizations. The goal is to continue cost reductions by increasing efficiencies. In conclusion, the main benefits of HR outsourcing include maintaining organizational control over the hiring process, application of purchasing capabilities for greater standardization in hiring processes pay rates and bill rates. So, any outsoucred HR organizations may be reduce hiring process cost.

Global outsourcing source strategy in a value supply chain

Why US organizations need to outsouce value supply chain to other countries logic organizations ?What is global outsourcing source strategy in a departmental role? In a highly competitive global environment, many manufacturers are responded by setting and outsourcing relations for components and finished products with lower cost producers on a contractual electronic commerce department, (original equipment manufacturer basis). Outsourcing strategy is part of the value supply chain of corporate activated. Nowadays, global outsourcing increases organizational and technological capacity of firms and cooperating a network of remotely located external suppliers performing. These understanding the important roles that product designers, engineers and production managers and purchasing manager etc. play in global sourcing strategy empowerment. Specially, electronic commerce is popular to supply chain. For example, Toyota car manufacturing company, owns unique capabilities by designing and manufacturing certain car components in-house , i.e. insourcing. Toyota also outsource manufacturing activities, Toyota adopts purchasing necessary, but no strategic inputs from independent component suppliers on obtaining a lower cost for these inputs. For example, products would be belts, tires and batteries to vehicle products that are not customized and do not differentiate its products from its competitors. Toyota's outsourcing strategy is car strategic inputs provide differentiation, e.g. engine, transmission etc. are sources from suppliers based on strategic partnership to gain to access to suppliers' capabilities and it is also a conceptualize global outsourcing sourcing strategy to Toyota car manufacturing company.

How value chain outsourcing affects firm level performance. Global outsourcing strategy means to identify which production units that will serve which particular markets and how components will be supplied for production and thus included a number of basic choices, companies can make in decision how to serve various markets. Either choice relates to the use of inputs, assembly or production within the country to serve a foreign market or decides to use of internal or external supplies of components or finished products. In this outsourcing source input situation, the term sourcing is needed to describe how multi-national companies mange in of components and finished products in serving foreign and domestic markets. Sourcing decision making is both contractual point of view, the sourcing of major components and products are occurred by multi-national companies. First is from parents or their foreign subsidiaries. Second is from independent suppliers on a contractual basis. The first type of sourcing is known as insourcing. Otherwise, the second type of sourcing is referred to outsourcing. How to achieve economies of scale by outsourcing or insourcing sourcing input strategy? Therefore, the two outsourcing strategies are multi-faceted and require careful examination.

Outsourcing benefits in economic view

What are benefits to US outsourcing organizations?The two economists (Abrahamson & Rosenkopf, 1993) indicated that In long term, outsourcing can help to reduce fixed investment in finance view point, in-house manufacturing facilities and thus lower the breakeven point, which subsequently helps boost an outsourcing company whose return on equity (ROE). Thus, if any one corporate performance is evaluated on the basis of its contribution to the company's ROE. Also, in the short term or long term on resource inputs outsourcing view, early adopters of outsourcing strategy indeed experienced efficiency gains as they were able to reduce fixed investment in in-house manufacturing facilities and lows their ROE. But, later adopters may have different to gain institutions legitimacy or because of competition pressures in the industry, despite some inherent uncertainties about the long term costs and benefits of outsourcing strategy. It seems that outsourcing strategy was devised as any organization's policy makers to access trade linkages of benefits for short term or long term. Outsourcing strategy is a systematic analysis of the economic, political and regulatory implications indicates potential benefits along with a number of potentially negative side effects to any organizations. Then, outsourcing strategy will be caused this question: How to assess the risks and benefits of outsourcing for organizational sectors and nations both? The decision to change outsourcing behavior to carry a business activity may have profound implications for outsourcer and outsource receiver both, but little impact of the sector level. The common occurrence of industry decisions to outsource most manufacturing, including sale of factories, it created a new sub-sector, contract manufacturing. Otherwise, at a national level and public sectors become less distinct to outsourcing strategy. Public policy on outsourcing has stimulated extensive debate, privatization social justice and value for money etc. challenges.

What motivate outsourcing what is being outsourced risk and concerns?

Whether what motivate outsourcing, evidence of what is being outsourced risk and concerns? Outsourcing activities include: outsources manufacturing components and other value adding activities. Some focused on employment is outsourced another firm's employees carrying out tasks previously performed one's own employees. Outsourcing is an activity outside the organization's chosen core competencies. It seems outsourcing is a sub-contracting relationships between firms, all foreign production, hiring of workers in non-traditional jobs, such as control workers and temporary and part time workers.

What are the motivations for outsourcing reasons? Why outsourcing is needed to any organization. For example, it can enable firms to focus on core activities. The concept of focus originates in operation on a small, manageable, number of tasks at which the operation becomes excellent to specific technologies and as a risk of vertical integration advantages. Other benefits of outsourcing appear is literature on strategic management, operations management, purchasing and supply and innovations. Moreover, outsourcing can improve flexibility to meet changing business conditions, demands for products, services and technologies by creating smaller and more flexible clear evidence includes improved creditability image, greater workforce flexibility and avoiding being backed into specific assets and technologies are harder to measure. How outsourcing can improve company performance. For airline manufacturing industry example, Hill & Jones (1995) showed that the manufacture of a large portion of the Boeing 767 is Boeing's third largest commercial aircraft, which is outsourced to Japanese manufacturers, which include Fuji, Kawasaki and Mitsubish. As a result, only 10% of the value of the 767 Boeing is produced in-house. So, outsourcing is an attempt to enhance manufacturing air place industry competitiveness.

How can choose smarter outsourcing

How US organizations can choose smarter outsourcing? Organizations hope to do sight options to save money, among themselves staff layoffs and a reduction of overhead costs, such as office space. Private companies have long outsourced in order to save time and money. During periods of economic growth, many organizations began to use outsourcing more frequently and staff workloads grew in proportion to increase budgets. Tasks such as conducting needs assessments, reviewing proposals, conducting site visits, monitoring and creating evaluations systems were increasingly given to outside contractors, consulting firms and independent consultants in the belief that external specialists could do the work more efficiently and effectively than company itself.

Nowadays, there is a growing stream of organizations need to research into the outsourcing of innovation activities within the innovation, management, marketing and economics disciplines. These organizations need to understand how with the outsourcing practice becoming more commonplace in their industry. However, their behaviors bring these two questions: Whether outsource or internalize innovation activities and the performance implications of this decision can support for both transaction cost and resource based arguments is examined with both theory bases showing substantial attention? Whether outsourcing innovation activities can lead to faster product development and cost savings? On advantages hand, it is possible that outsourcing may lead to higher costs and slower new product development. Further the technological uncertainty may have conflicting impacts on the outsourcing decision that are not yet well understand. When outsourcing product development has reduced costs and has proved speed to market. On disadvantages hand, outsourcing has also reduce product development time delays and higher quality concerns. Why to cause performance implications of outsourced innovation activities in transaction in cost economics and the resource-based view point? When outsourcing product development has been to reduce costs and has improved speed to market, outsourcing product development is not unlike other make or buy decisions. So, make vs buy decision is similar to logistic and IT outsourcing. Internalization of product development will be preferred when transaction costs are excessive. Otherwise, the market i.e. outsourcing will be selected when transaction costs are low. Transaction costs can include adaption, safeguarding and measurement costs. Adaption costs represent efforts to adjust contract to change conditions and are a result of environmental uncertainty. When a firm may have to revise on agreement with a partner company, this facing substantial penalties, due to an unstable market environments, the firm is likely to perform this function internally. Safeguarding costs characterize the costs of an outsourcing provider acting opportunities after investments have been made in the inter-firm relationship and are the result of transaction specific investment. Measurement costs include all expenses with confirming that contracts have been fulfilled passably. The contracting firm may face substantial costs to estimate quality for contractual services. When the sum total of these transaction costs is substantial, internalization will be favored.

What is environmental uncertainty factor?

Environmental uncertainty refers to unanticipated changes in circumstances surrounding an exchange in market uncertain and technological uncertainty. Market uncertainty is the fluctuation and unpredictability of demand. With respect to innovation projects, market uncertainty may cause frequent changes to the development, complications and adding expense to external contracting. These changes may necessitate renegotiation or cancellation of innovation contracts, which will likely carry prohibitive penalties (a term) transaction costs. These transaction costs promote internalization under high levels of market uncertainty. Otherwise, technological uncertainty environments, selecting market governance allows firms the flexibility to end relationship should technical requirements shift. It seems that market and technological external change factor will influence to benefits to any organizations to choose outsourcing strategy. On the other side, outsourcing can bring this question: Whether the offshore outsourcing of information technology jobs choice is suitable to any IT organizations? Nowadays. The offshore outsourcing if IT jobs from the United States has been enabled by a powerful influence of global economic demographic and technological forces. In fact, many IT companies were drawn to offshoring outsourcing because of the need for programmers to fix the Y2K problem in the late 1990- year. It is shortages of US programmers. Other factors driving this phenomenon include the wage gap between the US and developing countries, e.g. China and India, advances in technology, labor availability, expanding foreign markets and foreign government incentives. The spread of the offshoring phenomenon from low skill manufacturing to high wage white collar service industry jobs reduces the country's IT jobs critics, it represents the mobility for many US workers who saw post-secondary education as the route to a higher standard of living. The offshoring outsourcing of manufacturing and service jobs from the US to lower cost foreign nations become a national issue in a very short time. The impact of offshore outsource on the information technology sector gives outsourcing potential loss of millions of jobs at all wage levels and the critical contribution is the IT sector to US productivity growth. However, decisions about the locations of manufacturing or service facilities reflect market forces key factors include the size of local markets, capital availability and costs, labor availability skill levels and cost, logistic issues, reliability and infrastructure and IT in particular relationships with research institutions. All these factors will influence the choice of offshore outsource IT jobs strategy top any organizations.

outsourcing will bring what kind of work skills to US organization

Whether outsourcing will bring what kind of work skills. Many employers choose outsourcing to employ employees. This core of our work is identifying trends which will transform global society and the global marketplace. How it influences our nature of work form health care to technology, the work place and human identity. A decade ago, workers worried about jobs being outsourced overseas. Today companies, such as Odesk and Liveops can assemble teams " in the cloud" to dosales, customer support and many other tasks. It seems outsoucring can influence many high technological job of changes. Global connectivity, smart machines and new media are just some of the drivers reshaping how we thank about work, what constitutes work and the skills, we shall need to be productive contributors in the future. As computer technology in the cloud will be used popularly to society. A signal is typically a small or local innovation that has the potenial to grow in scale and geographic distribution. A signal can be a new product, a new practice, a new market strategy, a new policy or new technology, such as online cloud computing files storage service method. It is an innovative social science method to computer users. However, this new computer files storage method influences outsourcing service of needs increasing. It will have key drivers and skills areas that will be most relevant to the technological workforce of the future.

It is estimates that by 2025 year, the number of Americans over 60 age will increase by 70%. The challenge of an aging population will come. What it means to age, individuals will need to rearrange their approach to their career, family life and education to accommodate their life plan. Increasing, people will work long past 65 age in order to have adequate resources for retirement. Multiple careers will be commmplace and lifelong learning to prepare for occupational change will see major growth. To take advantage of this well experienced organizations will have to rethink the traditional career paths in organizations, creating more diversity and flexibility. As the high technological cloud computing storage method is invented. Any organizations can save their files to the central cloud computer storage system website to save or find their files from website more easily. It will reduce their computer department expenditure and staff salary. So, outsourcing computer file storage service demands will be influenced to increase to any organizations as well as organizations will reorganize their computer department job nature to shape the kinds of social, economic and political organizations which inhabit. Outsourcing is a good solve method to assist organizations to pay cheap salary to employ many retired high age workers by contract or temporary or part time method to reduce their computer department's number of employees and the retired labors only need to pay cheap salary to learn how to use internet to help whose employers to save their files to their outsourcing computer storage service provider's central computer storage system every day efficiently. So, organizations do not need to employ many computer department staffs to avoid to pay much salaries to this computer department expenditure. They can choose outsourcing to pay cheap salaries to employ many retirement labors to assist them to do simple office storage job from internet channel efficiently and effectively. Hence, internet high technological innovation can influence office outsoucing of job duties increasing.

Whether domestic outsoucing in the America, what assesses trends and effects on job quality. Nowadays, US firms' use of contractors and independent contractors and its effect on job quality and inequality. Why firms choose contract out for certain functions and assess their predictions about likely impacts on job quality, stagnant wages, growing inquality and the deterioration of job quality are among the most important challenges facing the US economy today. Although any country's domestic outsourcing , firms' use of contractors, franchises and independent contractors any one of these factors is a potentially important influence to companies reduce compensation and shift economy risk to workers. However, the domestic outsoucing takes place on a much larger scale and effects many more workers than has been recognized ranging from low wage service workers, security guards, warehouse workers and hotel housekeepers to professionals and technical workers, such as programmers, health care technicians and accountants. These tends are part of structural change in the organization of production to influence quality of jobs and the nature of employment contract after outsourcing jobs are popular. The quality of jobs include wages, benefits, employee skills and training and mobility opportunities and job security as well as inequality across jobs. Domestic outsoucing concerns these issues: such as employment and labor law, the provision of health, pension and other workplace benefits. However, any companies choose outsourcing of employment reasons include, such as that it relates how management choices to pursue value added or cost focused strategies. Contracting out is difficult to define because a large part ot economic activity has always occurred through business-to-business transactions, as captured in macro-economic input-output models. Outsoucing job employment method can influence any one labor's individual quality of jobs. Usually, international companies choose the offshoring of work in global supply chains. Until recently, the domestic counterpart outsourcing employment method has grown supply chains to domestic or regional outsoucing employment.

What factors cause domestic outsourcing and whether firm decisions about what to retain in-house and what to outsource have changes over time. Some evidence suggests that firms have responded by focusing on their core competencies and outsourcing low value added tasks as well as higher value added specialized functions. Advanced technologies have facilitated this process by allowing firms to outsource entire functions ans more easily monitor contractors as well as employees who work, leading to new forms of networked production and rise of specialized outsouring employment firms. Domestic outsoucing influences the changes of job quality, benefits, hours, workload, job stability, schedule stability and occupational safety, health, incidence of wage theft and access to training and promotions. Predictions are less clear for job requiring professional or technicial or specialized skills or those that are outsourced to large and diversified outsourced contractors. Types of outsourced contracts include: suppliers or vendors of products, such as manufacturing inputs or services, such as business services or staffs service or staffing firms, franchisees and independent contract, such as freelancers, independent contracts or non demand platform outsourced workers. It is significant restructuring of domestic manufacturing supply chains will greater reliance on suppliers and subcontractors. In addition, the potential growth of on demand outsourcing work as well as other forms of job fragmentation. It causes this question: How outsourced workers are multiple forms of income generating work to achieve economic security and how outsourcing workers can build career across jobs and over time.

Firm in every sector of the economy contract with other firms as part of their production process, as do governmental entities. The functions that are outsourced vary widely. For example: human resources ans research and development functions, building services, recycling, regulation and compliance, accounting, credit card collection, call centres, mortage and check processing, information technology and data processing, logistics and transportation, machine maintenance, cable installation, food services, food processing, parts manufacturing and assembly, laundry and housekeeping etc. outsourced jobs causes.

Whether what business impact of outsourcing will be caused? Nowadays, IT outsourcing was clearly a part of an effective management strategy that the companies felt IT outsourcing strategy can bring to achieve positive results. Information technology outsourcing providing servicers will be predicted to provide services that is expected to raise over the next five years minimum. The companies demand clients expected benefits of IT outsourcing and determined that cost reduction, increased operation, efficiency and improved IT effectiveness. What are the impacts of outsourcing to influence better long-term improvement in the business performance? It is impossible to being benefits of significant reduction and lower growth in sellings, general and administrative expense to IT outsourcing company demand clients. Also, pre-existing corporate cultures are focused on business improvement to IT outsourcing company demand clietns. In the past researches, some economists indicated that points can be used to reflect the actual numbers increase or decrease in percent. However, their prior researches shows that prior to outsourcing, the annual growth in selling, general and administration expenses of eompanies in the study was already 4.2 points lower than sector medium. Moreover, within one to two years after IT outsourcing these companies improved even most. Annual growth in selling and general administrative expenses for them was 9.9 points lower efford to assist any IT outsourcing will have selling and administrative expenses for long term. Also, almost two-third of the companies studied outperformed in increased growth in return on asset two to three years after IT outsourcing commenced. Prior to outsourcing, the annual ROA growth rate for companies in the study ws 7.5 points lower than the sector median. After outsourcing, however these companies experienced 8.6 points higher median a substantial change of 16.1 points. Also, nearly two to third of the companies studied grew earnings faster than their peers. Two to three years after IT outsourcing, companies experienced an annual rate of growth in earnings 11.8 points higher than the growth rate of the sector median. Thus, it seems IT outsourcing can assist the IT outsourcing demand clients to reduce expenditure and to raise income both as the same time. Then, it will cause these questions to IT outsourcing demand clients. Is outsourcing influencing in an economic downturn to finance sector in the short term? Is the finance sector's renewed change for outsourcing just a temporary cost-cutting measure? Will today's economic climate initiate long term financial and productivity gains? Whether what are benefits and disadvantages of outsourcing finance sector IT. I shall demonstrate why outsourcing open source software support and maintenance can be a good choice to start. Firstly when company plans to budget cuts expenditures, IT outsourcing is often the first choice. For example in 2003 year, Zurich Financial services' sprawling IT department consisted of more than 7,500 employees. After posting a record loss of 3.4 billion the year before, Zurich decided to cut down on in those staff and outsource nearly half of its IT work. Outsourcing has successfully cut costs by 45 percent and cut the number of in house IT staff by 60 percent. Here are some of the benefits that companies enjoy when they outsource information technology functions to competent, reliable vendors.

In fact, it can be too expensive to maintain, company's own information technology, especially during a recession. Fortunately, many IT functions can be easily and efficiently outsourced, positively impacting individual company's bottom line. Employee costs are much higher than just salary and benefits, keeping employees happy, productive and busy takes time, effort and money. Although, many IT staffs will be dismissed, it will increase the unemployment ratio in societies. But, moving an IT service out of house means financial organizations don't have to worry about technology refresh costs in the future. It also cuts down on human resources requirements, specialist IT service provides which can provide the newest technologies and deliver quality service more than company itself in house information provides are the most effective to develop and implement and upgrade their clients' software or the launch on a new platform, due to the expert's time is wasted on day-to-day duties for whose other IT outsourcing demand clients. However, instead of IT outsourcing service outsourced offshoring in that service sector, how economic impact to influence the outsourced offshoring country. For example, United States continues to run an international trade surplus in services. Many Americans are particularly concerned about the loss of skilled, well paid jobs in such fields as computer programming and accounting etc. positions. These jobs seemed relatively secure at a time when many manufacturing jobs were being cost to import competition. Similarly, telephone call centers, once viewed as an esonomic development opportunity in some areas, increasingly are moving low wage countries, such as India and the Philippines. Thus, offshoring raises many questions for policymakers and general public. For example, which service jobs will be affected most by import competition. What are the likely effects of service-sector offshoring on U.S.A. output, employment and our standard of living, such as America? Is offshoring really a problem that requires restrictive government actions or are other kinds of policies more appropriate to give Americans or other countries the highest possible living standard?

The term of offshoring refers to the relocation of jobs and production to a foreign country. The relocated jobs and production could be at a foreign office of the same multinational company or at a separate company located abroad. In constrast, the term outsourcing doesn't necessary imply that jobs and production are relocated to another country. The major outsourcing service jobs include human resource, accounting and information technology etc. in-house service jobs in large organizations. However, the loss of service jobs and factory production is caused by offshoring is diffuclt to measure. It is also difficult to determine the impact of offshoring on total services employment in the United States or other countries. International trade in services covers a wide range of industries and activites. For example, travel and transportation includes travel expenditures, passenger fares and frieght and port services, royalties and license fees cover transactions including patents, copyrights, trademarks and other intangible proprietary rights to use, produce or distribute products. Other private services include many of these industries, such as education, financial services insurance, telecommunications and other professional services etc. Some economists indicated that occupational employment statistics for the Unisted States provided additional evidence that past service sector offshoring had been small. About 14 million service jobs were at risk of offshoring in 2000 year, when about 96 million service jobs had a low risk of ofshoring. The decline in the at-risk service occupations from 2000 year to 2002 year was about 218,000 jobs or roughly 109,000 jobs annually, relatively small number that is consistent with the estimates of McCarthy or Zandi. In percentage terms, employment in the at risk occupations fell at a faster rate from 2000 year to 2002 year than in the low risk occupations. This faster decline is consistent with offshoring activity, although the decline is consistent with other explanations as well, such as faster of technological change in industries employing the risk occupations or greater cyclical sensitivity in these industries. Because offshoring was not the only cause of job loss in the risk occupations, the number of jobs moved offshore was undoubtedly less than 109,000 jobs annually. However, the estimates may understate the total impact because domestic companies with expanding worldwide employment may have located may of their newly created jobs abroad even when they didn't reduce their US employment. Some of those foreign jobs might provide services to US customers and potentially foreign jobs might provide service to US . Conversely, the estimates may overstate the total job loss from offshoring of the foreign outsourcing of some support jobs prevents the loss of other domestic jobs by keeping US firms competitive in world markets. For example, cost reductions from offshoring IT jobs might help a US financial services company win foreign contracts, preserving many professionals and support jobs in the US.

Lower production costs in foreign countries are a major cause of service sector offering. Although, the costs of land and other resources may be cheaper abroad, but the main difference betweeb the US and developing countries is labor costs. There is a large gap in computer programmer wages between the US and other countries. Any organizational capital includes both physical capital, such as machinery and computers and human capital , such as skills and knowledge. The cost savings is come from offshoring also might be reduced if the firm needed to pay higher transportation and telecommunication costs or management spends more time on service quality and data security. Still, the much lower levels of wages ans benefits in developing countries suggests that many services can be produced abroad at lower cost. The in-house professional relocation of labor-intensive service activities, such as legal transcription services to countries with lower labor costs is consistent with economists' basic theory of international trade, comparative advantage. So, in-house outsourced professional service will be a corporative advantage, if the country's legal profession is poor level to compare with the another country. e.g. the skill in-house the legal professional labors of the developing country, such as China is poor educational level to compare with the developed country, such as US. So, if China large organizations chose to outsource themselves in-house legal service jobs to outsource offshoring to US legal professional lawyers to do. It can bring comparative advantage to China large outsourced in-house legal service organizations, due to these China outsourced large organizations can reduce to employ to pay too much salaries to these many in-house Chinese domestic lawyers and the US outsourced legal consultants whose can give more professional legal recommendation to serve to the China large organizations.

In conclusion, although offshoring strategy can increase unemployment chance for this disadvantge. But, all of outsourcing benefits weighs are more than the offsourcing disadvantages. However, outsourcing strategy can have these benefits to the outsourced service demanders. Such as outsourcing is no longer just about cost saving, it is also a strategic tool that may power the twenty first century global economy. Moreover, outsourcing can increase productivity and competitiveness, e.g. for every 1000 jobs British Airways sends to India , the airline saves $23 million, companies can devote a portion of their outsourcing savings to helping employees make job transitions, also leader can no longer afford to view outsourcing as a business tactic, it is now essential to remain competitive. On the world stage, workers now compete globally, so individuals must continually learn more to vie successfully with their peers worldwide, the average company only spends about 20% of the value of its outsourcing contracts to manage its relationship with the outsource provider. So, in the positive view point, outsourcing strategy can bring a potential primary driver of the global economy development. Although, outsourcing can also cause the raising of domestic unemployment chance. But companies may soon be more outsourced than in sourced, signifying a fundamental reorganization that will affect employees, managers, customers and executives. Customers' choice will increase product costs will drop and workers' roles will change. Finally, the most important, the developing country will earn comparative advantage from the developed country's employers' offshoring jobs provision. Thus, the developing country's unemployment rate will be reduced, then the global economy will be kept more balance fairly.

Global outsourcing competition influences to cause wealth inequality

Globalization brings international trade dramatically in recent decades and flows of products and services are important for achieving economic growth in development countries. However, in parallel with increasing global interconnections, progress toward world poverty is at the center of global development policy and research. Whether the super rich country, America can control globalization to influence wealth inequality. Despite the significant advancement in measuring poverty and income distribution which is limited to regard the impact to different economic policy both national and international on poverty outcomes. So whether can global competition influence wealth inequality in the world?

The super rich America which had been achieving foreign direct investment flows typically follow trade liberalization to different Asia countries, e.g. China. It invested to build many factories in China to employ cheaper China domestic labors to substitute to build factories to employ

America domestic labors in America. The reason is because the China foreign labors of costs can be reduced very much to compare to employ America domestic labors for long term for America any businesses. Although, it seems that it can reduce China unemployment ratio. But, it seems that it can influence wealth inequality, due to America employers choose not to employ many domestic manufacturing labors who had been working in their current employer to earn incomes to support their life in America. So, this suddenly unemployment changing will influence many America manufacturing labors can not find another kind of same jobs easily in America. Due to there are many skillful manufacturing workers supply, but there are not many manufacturers demand, so this suitation cause them to feel difficult to find the same kind of manufacturing job nature to work in America very easily. To conclude, America manufacturing labor unemployment ratio will be raised. Moreover, many America manufacturing sectors of employers who need to pay much wages to China manufacturing labors, the America wealth will transfer to China to raise China GDP (Gross product production) income, per capita China individual manufacturing labor income. But, America the labor group's wealth will be reduced and the America GDP and per capita America individual income will be also reduced in society. I think the America employers' choice of foreign outsourcing employment issue will reduce America overall manufacturing labor individual wealth (capita per income) to be transferred to the other developing countries, e.g. China. It will cause China overall manufacturing labor individual wealth to be increased. So, it means that America employers' choice of foreign outsourcing employment issue will be influenced to America wealth inequality in itself country. Otherwise, it will influence China manufacturing labor group's wealth will be increased.

However, some economists indicate that the number of individuals living on less than USD$2.00 a day which can define poverty. In fact, some countries are encountering poverty challenge. For example, India still has many people whose have no more than USD$2.00 to support their living nowadays. So, it finds that income distribution is inequality or is equally conflicting in India.

Since 1980 year, America had become one developed country and its overall country economic growth or GDP income was the highest and per capital income or individual family income was also higher to compare other countries in the world. Otherwise, despite the relatively glowing of changing nature of income distribution to other developing countries. e.g. China, India which wealth inequality remains excessive until today. Even though, the debate on whether inequality has increased or has decreased over time remains unsolved, these developing countries' wealth inequality still remain high in the world. For example, the average levels of poverty head count and inequality in developing countries, e.g. India, China, Korea over 80 percent of the population is living at USA$2.00 a day to support their life, it means that who are poor to live in these developing countries.

In global competition, it includes that super rich country America anticipates, whether globalization will cause wealth inequality within and across nations, due to America anticipation. Supposing to the changes in per capita income are the main determinants of changes in poverty to wealth inequality in the world. But maximizing per capita income of fast global competition might not place sufficient weight on poverty and inequality reduction. The differences within and between countries inequality is an issue in the arguments on the impact of global competition. In special, America is the main player who decides to participate to global competition. Also, since 1980 year, America self country's economy had been beginning to grow high every year. Whether had America caused consequences to influence wealth inequality between other countries and within itself country income distribution, as well as poverty to cause wealth inequality in the world? Thus, to answer this question, it is important to confirm that it has relationship between poverty and wealth inequality and global competition to judge whether America can influence wealth inequality in the world finally. So, it seems that either the super rich country America can not influence wealth inequality in the world if it has been confirmed to have no any relationship between poverty and wealth inequality and global competition, due to America decides to participate to global competition. Otherwise, or America can influence wealth inequality in the world if it has been confirmed to have any relationship between poverty and wealth inequality and global competition.

Relationship between US outsourcing competition and wealth inequality

A key issue in the debate about global competition in general is the extent to which economic growth reduces poverty. If economic growth is to benefit everyone proportionally, the incomes of the poor would grow at the same rate as mean income. However, if economic growth in poverty reduction will be less(or more) depending in whether the incomes of the poor grow by less(more) than average. For example, Hong Kong, China,

India, those developing countries still have many people (householders) are living of the poverty line, who do not earn enough income to support their families' living every day. Although, these countries' governments have social welfare to assist them and these countries seem their GDP incomes are growing up every year. But it is not enough to support them because the inflation will be raised every year for long term as well as there are many poor people are living in the poor housing environment due to who have not effort to pay rent or to buy house, no enough education fees to support them children to go to school to study between primary and tertiary stages, no enough saving to prepare retirement.

Whether it has the linkage between global competition and poverty to cause these developing countries' wealth inequality in the world. We can focus on two measures of global competition's trade and international capital flows. Globalization produces both winners and losers among the poor in the world. In fact, some poor individuals are made worse off by trade or financial integration to get support as income support from the governments, e.g. corn farmers in Mexico, China, food aid in India, China and other appropriately design social safety nets to accompany trade reforms. Also, America had been anticipating to global competition, it had affected different aspects of poverty in developing countries. It seems America's anticipation to global competition will be raised the openness growth link by these factors mobility such as related changes in global markets and power structures, changes in relative products and factor prices, changes the nature of technical progress and the technological process, changes terms of trade, affecting both the demand for exports and supply capacity, impact on the flow of information, global disinflation, i.e. the decline in inflation across countries' influencing the developing countries, e.g. Hong Kong, China, Korea, India etc. and developed countries, e.g. England, France, Germany, Japan, New Zealand, Australia etc. To mediate the effects and various channels to link global competition and income distribution poverty. It seems wealth inequality and poverty both are caused by global competition between developed and developing countries. If they have had direct relationship, whether the super rich country America had participated global competition between developing and developed countries in these different sectors , such as international trading, space science, medical science, weapon production etc. Has it enough ability to influence these countries' wealth inequality? In the another view point, these countries would not encounter wealth inequality if America did not participate the global trade competition. We need to judge the wealth inequality would not be caused if the global competition was only between the developing countries and the developed countries which particpate, excluding the America's participation.

In the history, economic inequality had been increasing in much of the industrialized world, but United States is unusual in the relatively high levels of inequality and the power reserved to its subnational governments. Using power resources framework, America government has ability to enact policies to reduce wealth inequality in itself country. However, some economists see inequality as a natural product of a market economy that is unimportant relative to outcomes like economic growth and poverty, when others see wealth inequality as a social ill in itself. So, it seems America had no any ability to cause wealth inequality issue occurrence to other countries before the industrialization stage passed. Although, it seems that America employers' choice of outsourcing foreign manufacturing labor strategy will influence itself country's manufacturing labor individual per capita income reduction to cause income inequality in itself country. But it is not represent that America had ability to influence wealth inequality to influence the world after it was one main player to participate the global competition in possible. So, it seems that the world's wealth inequality challenge is not influenced by America's participation to global competition when it was also one main player for the reason. Also it seems that the America's participation to global competition is not the main factor to cause these countries themselves wealth inequalities. It ought have other factors to cause the wealth inequality in the world. I shall indicate some of other factors which can influence wealth inequality in possible, such as below:

Does US outsoucing strategy influence wealth inequality?

In the first view point factor is such as the extreme inequalities in incomes and assets has been caused to developed and developing both countries. For example, developed countries, e.g. France, Japan, Australia, England etc. developing countries, e.g. China, Hong Kong, Korea, India etc. These countries' employers had paid whose high level of management staff salary is very high and this management level of staff salary will be increased every year. Otherwise, these countries employers also paid whose middle and low both levels staff are very low and these both levels staff whose salary won't be increased very easily every year, even, they will be unemployed if their employers faced financial challenges. Moreover in general, developing or developed countries which governments like to raise salary to the high management level public servant staffs easily. Otherwise, which won't like to raise salary to low or/and middle both levels public servant staffs every year easily. So, it will cause the public servant staff range is very high between the management level public servant staff and the low and middle levels public servant staff and any of these countries' government had done the unfair public servant salary review to treat to their low and middle level staffs in their countries every year for long term. It seems that America's participation to global competition will not influence any one of these countries' wealth inequality directly. So, it seems that the unfair salary review and wealth inequality of treatment issues will be caused to any one country in the world, even the global competition will not be caused, due to America's participation. So, it seems that any country's employers and governments which unfair salary review will be one factor to influence the wealth inequality to themselves.

In the another view point factor, I also argue the relationship between development countries and gender inequality why which can be explained by the process of development and society-specific factor to cause the wealth inequality by themselves. For example, China and India that have many people are poor today or at least some of them have cultural features that exacerbate favoritism toward males. Being poor is insufficient to explain parent's strong desire to have a son in China and India in custom. In past, the effects of gender inequality can influence economic development to these any of developing countries. More gender inequality causes wealth inequality in these any one of countries, e.g. China, India. In fact, poor countries have no a monopoly on gender inequality. Men earn more than women in essentially all societies. However, disparities in health, education and bargaining power within marriage tend to be larger in countries with low GDP per capita. Moreover, the education gender inequality is also be caused to these poor countries. A negative relationship between the schooling gender gap and GDP is also for primary, secondary and tertiary school enrollment stages. Such as the male student enrollment number is often more than the female student enrollment number of primary, secondary and tertiary schools to these any one of countries, such as China, Korea, India every year. So, these poor countries' male gender graduate students' income and male gender student enrollment number will be higher than the female gender graduate student's income and female gender student enrollment number every year for long term. Due to the high education graduates of the male gender is more than the female gender to these any one of countries every year. So, it will cause high wealth inequality between male and female graduate gender in these countries. It means that male average salary will be higher than female average salary in these countries, due to the male student enrollment number will be high than female student enrollment number in order to cause the male graduate student number will be higher in these countries every year. It seems that these countries' gender inequality factor can cause the male and female themselves income inequality, then it can cause male and female wealth inequality in these countries. So, it seems that it has no any relationship between the America's participation to global competition and the gender inequality to cause wealth inequality to these countries.

To conclude, the causing of the world's wealth inequality's main factor is not come from the America's participation to global competition. It ought be the other both factors, such as themselves gender inequality factor and these countries themselves employers and governments unfair and unreasonable salary review factor which influence the wealth inequality to themselves.

However, due to US encouraged outsourcing strategy to achieve to global businesses development in popular. Moreover, many global businessmen choose to dismiss their employees, then which let outsourced providers to help them to choose the suitable outsourced employees to do any company internal departments' job. So, outsourcing can also cause large number of unemployment. It will raise the upper managment and low(floor) labors their income distance very much. For long term, the global wealth inequality will be rasied. Hence, outsouring is the main factor to cause global wealth inequality.

CHAPTER TWO

Outsourcing brings social behavioral economic benefit

- What does behavioral economy mean?
- (BE) Behavioral economics is primarily concerned with the bounds of rationality of economic agents. Behavioral models typically bring insights from psychology and microeconomic theory. The study of behavioral economics includes how market decisions are made and the mechanisms that drive public choice. Moreover, behavioral economic plays a important role in our lives and in the economy because it can help businesses to explain why we consume the kind of goods and services , the way we do, why we make certain choices of action, the key contibution to behavioral economics, it uses psychological and experimentation to develop theories about human decision making, and has identified a range of biases as a result of the way people think and feel . (BE) is trying to change the way economics think about people's perception of value and expresses preferences.

● Have they relationship between consumer behaviors and economy ?
The success or failure of a nation's economy can greatly affect consumer behavior based on a variety of economic factors. If the economy is strong, consumers have more purchase power and money is spent , f the economy is poor, the reverse is true. Consumer behavior in economics means to explain of how individual cstomers, groups or organizations select, buy, use and dispose ideas, goods and services. A such, consumers play a vitual role in the economic system of a capitalist economy. Without consumer demand, producers would lack one of the key motivations to produce to sell to consumers.

The motivates consumers behavioral economic perspective, it is the new field of behavioral economics has shown them, in practice, people's decisions can be greatly influenced by seemingly irrelevant aspects of their personalities and by the environment in which their decisions are made. So, it seems that consumer buying behavior changes during economic crisis.

In organization how resources choices to use in behavioral economy view, though the number and variety of the different resources businesses require is limitless. Economists divide factors of production into three basic categories: Land, labour and capital. Land refers to all of the natural resources that businessed need to make and distribut goods and services, labours to make and distribute goods and services, labours refers how the organization chooses to employ the employee skill to make the kind of job, capital refers to how much the organization plans to spend in order to operate its business. Hence, behavioral economy can explains the economic model of employee, human behavior, working performance. It is a representation of people action. The concept is based on traditional economics, where human behavior is believed to spring from absolute rationality.

On behavioral economics in consumer lives and in the economy aspect, it explains it is a game theory, behavioral game theory. It is a game theory , behavioral game theory extened standard analytical game theory by taking into account how players (consumers) feel about the payoffs other players receive, limits in strategic thinking, as well as the effects of learning , the consumer individual past purchase experience, games (choices of purchases) are usually about cooperation or fairness.

For advertising how plays beneficial roles in a healthy economy example, advertising plays a strong role in the economy. It provides useful informatin to consumers that tells them about products and services choices as well as comparing features, benefits and prices, with more complete information, consumers and businesses often choose to purchase additional products and services . Hence, behavioral eonomics draws instead on psychology and economics to explore why people sometimes make irrational decisions, and why and how their behavior does not follow the predictionsof economic models. Because humans are emotional and easily distracted being, they make decisions that are not in their self-interest. So, behavioral economics is the study of the effects that psychological factors have on the economic decisions making process of individuals. The importance of understanding behavioral economics for marketers is immeasurable as it shows for a better factors that can lead to irrational economic decision, e.g. overspend because of lack of availabiliey, such as buying expense gad because you are in the desert. Another irrational economic decision may be impluse buying or pressure.

● How to apply behavioral economic to explain why the employee does peformance behavior?

A study on human behavior has revealed that 90% of the working population can be classified into four basic personality types: Optimistic, pessimistic, trusting. However, the latter of the four types. Envious is the most common, with 30% compared to 20% of each of the organization whole employee individual economic behavior, economic behavior occurs in a climate of formal and informal organizational rukes. These rules often act as incentives, e.g. appreciation, job promotion, increasing salary. These rules often act as incentives and influence the choices employees make , in general employees chooce to work desk jobs that do not keep to fit, and how they have to make more time to stay healthy.

So, behavioral economic theory explain any organization will need have behavioral skills to dominate employee individual performance to raise. Behavioral skills are interpersonal, self-regulatory, and task-related behaviors that connect to successful performance in education and workplace settings. The behavioral skills are designed to help individuals succeed thorough effecttive interactions, stress management and persistent effort in any organizations. for task-oriented behavioral skills examples, they may include: active always buy with something, ambitious, strongly wants to succeed, cautious, being very careful, conscientious, taking time to do things right and creative, someone who can make up things easily or think of new things. The six important employee behaviors in organizations are employee productivity, absenteeism, turnover, organizational citizenship behavior, job satisfaction and workplace misbehavior. So, managers need have good behavioral management skills. They are all about learnings appreciation and growth. Take the time to learn, try and grow oen strategies and leadership style.

● How to apply behavioral eocnmic skill to help society to solve challenges ?

The three principles of social economics theory describes how the economy as a whole woks are (1) a country's standard of living depends on its ability to produce goods and services . (2) prices rise when the government prints too much money and (3) society faces a short-run tradeoff between inflation and unemployment. How to use behavioral economics for social impact. According to the American psychological association, social psychology is the study of how individuals affects and are affected by physical environment. Behavioral economics applies these concepts to the economic decisions that people make in addition to the ration thinking. It helps us understand how consumer participate in contest buy products and brand familiar choice in order to make the most rational purchase decison. Also, behavioral economists ask questions mostly about the way people make economic choices, judgements or the way particular financial purchase choice.

Hence, behavioral economic is the study of psychology as it relates to the economic decision making processes of individuals and organizations. In general, our societies ask two important questions: Are economists' assumptions of utility of profit maximization good approximations of real people's behavior? So individuals maximize subjective expected utility?

IN our societies, we need to satisfy and earn the greatest benefit, in economics, rational choice theory, states that when humans are presented with various options under the conditions of scarcity, they would choose the option that maximizes their individual satisfaction. Behavioral economics draws on psychology and economics to explain why people sometimes make irrational decisions and why and how their behavior does not follow the predictions of economic models, e.g. decisions such as how much to pay for a cup of coffee, whether to go to graduate school, whether to pursue a healthy lifestyle , how much to contribute toward retirement. For example, humans are emotional and easily distracted beings, they make decisions that are not in their self interest. For companies are increasingly incorpoarting behavioral economics to incrase sales of their products case example, in 2007, the price of the 8 GB iphone was introduced for $600 and quickly reduced to $400, what if the intrinsic value of the phone was

$400? If Apple introduced the iphone for $400, the initial reaction the price in the smartphone market might have been negative as the iphone might be thought to have too pricely. Buy by introdicing the phone at a hgh-pricing and bringing it down to $400, consumers believed they were getting a pretty iphone deal for Apple. So, Apple iphone began to understand tht its phone consumers are irrational, an effective way to behavioral economics in thc Apple iphone's decision making policies that concern its internal and external stakeholders may prove to be worthwhile of done properly .

- Behavioral economics is the study of the psychological, cognitive, emotional, cultural and social factors involved in the decisions of individuals or institutions, and how these decisions deviate from those implied by classical economic theory.

-

- Behavioral economics is grounded in empirical observations of human behavior, which have demonstrated that people do not always make what neoclassical economists consider the "rational" or "optimal" decision, even if they have the information and the tools available to do so.

- Behavioral economics combines elements of economics and psychology to understand how and why people behave the way they do in the real world. It differs from neoclassical economics, which assumes that most people have well-defined preferences and make well-informed, self-interested decisions based on those preferences.

- Behavioral economics is often related with normative economics. It draws on psychology and economics to explore why people sometimes make irrational decisions, and why and how behavior diverges from the predictions of economic models. Behavioral economics is the study of psychology that analyzes the economic decisions people make. Moreover, behavioral economics explains that humans are not rational and are incapable of making good decisions. Because humans are emotional and easily distracted beings, they make decisions that are not in their self-interest.

Consumer leisure need whether is more and less whether it has what relationship between economy?

Consumer leisure need whether is more and less whether it has what relationship between economy? Also whether the country's economy recession or growth, can it influence consumer leisure need to increase or decrease ? I shall attempt to apply behavioral economy theory to explain whether they have cause and effect relationship as below:

In our societies, there are so many different kinds of leisure activities, also any kinds of leisure consumers can follow the kind of leisure activity's price factor, enjoyable feeling factor, satisfactory feeling factor, lesiure time need factor to influence the leisure consumer individual final choice to which kind of leisure activity among the different kinds of leisure needs. For example, travel leisure activity ought be the most experience, spending of leisure expense to compare general sport lesiure, e.g. swimming , playing basketballs , table tennis, tennis, football, purchae tickets seeing movies, purchase tickets listening music, purchase electronic playing games to stay at homes to play.

In simiarity, it uses only considers leisure price aspect, we shall do the comparable and reasonable decision is that travelling activity ought be the kind of leisure activity, any leisure consumers ought spend the least leisure times to enjoy this kind of leisure activity, e.g. one year has only one time or two-to-five times for overseas for overseas travel. But, in fact, in global there are many travellers, they can make many times of travelling frequent decision, e.g. they can spend one week at least time to go to overseas to travel per month. Hence, it means that global some travellers like to buy air ticket to go to overseas to travel, they spend average one month and one time overseas travel.

In fact, tourism agents hope to attract travellers to choose travelling leisure activity, they will attempt to decrease air ticket price in order to increase travellers number. However, some cheap travelling package price can persuade global some travellers accept to pay cheap price to bu air ticket to spend several days to go to the country to travel enjoy their holidays.

So, it seems that cheap air tcket price strategy, it can attract some countries travellers to accept to spend some time for their overseas holiday their overseas travelling leisure activity can explain why leisure price must be main element factor to influence leisure consumers to reduce spending amount to pay for the kind of leisure activity , such as travelling lesiure activity is one kind of good lesiure activity example.

Otherwise, some kinds of leisure activities, ever their lesiure prices are cheap, it must not influence them to like to spend much time to enjoy them, e.g. swimming, riding bicycles leisure activities, although those kinds of sport leisure activities prices must be very cheap to compare travelling activities , it can must influence many young people like to buy bicycles to ridem even they are proficient bicycle riders or they like to buy tickets to go public swimming pools to swin. The factors may include these both kinds of sports are tired sport leisures, any one must need more body energy to do these sports. Moreover, for student leisure consumers, although these both kinds sports prices, such as bicycles and swimming pool purchase tickets, they are cheap to students, but in fact, students must need to spend time to learn, if they often spend time to enjoy these both of sport activities, they will feel fear that they can not concentrate on spending learning time, if they spend on sport leisure time.

Hence, in behavioral economy view, it explains that lesiure price whether it is high or low, it is not main factor to influence any leisure consumers to do leisure kind of choice, such as sport case to student leisure consumers, they will not choose to spend much time on sport lesiure aspect, because the hard students must feel fear to influence their learning effort when they often spend time on sport leisure aspect. Otherwise, for a sport professonal, e.g. proficient riding bicycle sportman, he may accept to spend expensive price to buy one expensive bicycle , e.g. when he feels the US$3,000 bicycle, it can help him to improve riding speed skills, he won't choose to buy the another US$1,000 bicycle, when he feels that it can not help him to improve riding speed skill, hence, it also explains that the leisure produt high price , it must not influence lesisure consumers number to reduce, it depends on whether the leisure product function to the leisure consumer, e.g. for riding bicycle sport men , they may accept to pay higher price to buy more expensive bicycles , because the hope that the bicyces can help them to comprove their riding speed to more rapid. Otherwise, for student bicycle consumers, they won't compare different kinds of bicycles prices in order to decide whether which kind of bicycles are the most suitable to them to buy to ride. Hence, behavioral economic theory can explain that price must not be the main factor to influence lesiure consumers' lesiure activities choices, their lesiure need psychological and leisure product individual function factors was also influence their lesiure activities choices.

● Can DNA reproductive technology bring only positive impact to influence our social behavior change?

Human's medical technology had been continue developed to improve to satisfy our medical need, such as cancer patient medical different new drug research, it aims to help future cancer patients to avoid death. However, future human's new medical research will research on DNA biological medical improvement . So, future DNA biological medical technology may bring good or bad social impact, e.g. reproductive animal, such as pig, cow animals . So, when many pigs and cows can be reproduced. Then, pigs and cows number can increase. Consequently, porks beefs meats food number can be also been increased by DNA biological medical reproductive cell technology improvement.

It is good aspect to bring enough meats supply to global , when future DNA biological medical technology can be developed to the reprodctive many cows and pigs number stage in order to raise porks and beefs food number. However, DNA biological cell reproductive technology can also bring bad impact to our society, if one day human can apply DNA biological cell reprodutive technology to reproduce another ourselves, it means that reproductive human why is it bad new? if ne DNA scientist decides to help one country ambitious leader to reproduce himself, then when the country ambitious leader dies, but his another reproductive himself person can aontiue to bring war crisis to global, such as Japan's past leader, he was one ambitious leader to dominate global countries. If DNA reproductive technology is applied to help him to reproduce this Japan ambitious another himself . Then, the another new world war may be occurred easily. So, I also worry about future DNA reproductive technology may be applied to help the ambitous bad people to reproduce themselves to bring our societies safety and economic recession negative impact.

So, it brings this question: Can DNA reproductive technology bring only positive impact to influence our social behavior change? I shall attempt to explain as below:

How does DNA attract our behavior? In some situations, genes play a larger role in determining your behavior. How can genetic technologies impact society ? Although, genetic technology has a great potential to change the medical practice as we know it also has a potential to be misused , it also has a potential to be misused, and lead to further health disparities, discrimination and inequality in the human societies around the world.

However, I believe that those the ways that genetic engineering can help human society. Several works have been done on genetic engineering with major focus on its importance ranging from increasing plant and animal food productio, diagnosing disease condition, medical treatment improvement, as well as production of vaccines and other useful drugs.

● What is the focus of behavioral generics?

Behavioral genetics is the study of genetic and environmental influences on behaviors. By examining genetic influence, more information can be gleaned about how the environment operates to affect behavior. So, in behavioral economic view, gene DNA reproductive cell technology may seem to bring these benefits. Some benefits of genetic engineerinf in agricultures are increased crop yoelds, reduced need for food or drug production, reduced need for pesticides, enhanced nutrient composition and food quality , resistance to past and disease , greater food security, and medical benefits to the world's growing population . Also, the intangible , non economic measurement, possible benefit of genetic engineering may include more nutritious food, tastier food, disease -and-drought resistant plants that require fewer environment resources , such as water and fertilizers, less use of pesticides, increased supply of food with reduced cost and larger shelf life, faster growing plants and animals.

All of these benefits, they can not measured by economic calculation, but they can be felt by us. So, in our social behevioral economic view to genetic engineering, it may bring both positive and negative impact to our societies. On negative impact, these are many risks involves in genetic engineering, the release of genetically altered organisms in the environment can increase human suffering, disease animal welfare, and lead to ecological disasters are positive impact aspect, it can help to defeat diseases, getting rid of all illnesses in young and unborn children potential to live longer, produce new foods, organisms can be tailor-made , faster growth in animals and plants, pests and diseases resistance. But genetic engineering can also bring risks to our societies, e.g. new allergens in the food supply, antibiotic reistance, production of new toxins, concentration of toxic metals, enhancement of the environment for toxic fungi, unknown harms, gene transfer to wild ot weedy relations, change in herbicide use patterns.

By knocking out genes repsonsible for certain conditions, it is possible to create animal model organism of " human disease" as well as producing hotmenes, vaccies and other drugs. So, if DNA can bring human diseases, it means that it can also bring economic loss to our societies, because human disease may bring illness to any one to cause low productivity to any industry development, if the factory has many people human disease from reproductive animal cell accident risk. Then, the ill worker number increases, low productivities and inefficiencies will cause to the factory. If global has many factory workers got human disease from reproductive animal cell accidently. Then, global factries products producing number must have been influenced to fallen down.

Consequently, global manufacturers will encountered serious loss, due to their products producing speed is slow and their different kinds of products supply number must decrease, if global will workers number increases, they are caused by reproductive animal cell disease. Hence, DNA genetic reproductive technology may also bring global economic loss crisis in possible.

In organizational behavioral economic view, whether they have cause and effect relationship between employees how to use resources behaviors and organizational resource excess use within organizations ?
In organizational behavioral economic view, whether they have cause and effect relationship between employees how to use resources behaviors and organizational resource excess use within organizations. For example, if the organization has many employees number, whether the organization will use its any internal tangible and intangible resources easily per day.

For construction organization example, one construction organization must need to buy different kinds of construction materials to prepare to let workers to help it to manufacture different kinds of properties or houses (products) in order to sell to property buyers. In its every building construction site, it will need more or less workers, they are needed to use different kinds of construction materials to build housess in different construction sites. I assume that construction site (A), it has 100 construction workers number, every day, construction site (A) 100 workers need to use different kinds of construction materials to help them to build 3 building floors wall at least floor number in the construction site (A).

I assume that these 100 construction workers , they include proficient workers and not proficient workers. For proficient construction workers group, they have 50 number, and not proficient construction workers group, they also have 50 number . Hence, the proficient construction workers only need to spend 3 hours maximum and use less number of constructoin materials, then they can finish to build 3 building floors wall per day.

I also assume that all constructoin material supply number is limited. It means that due to this construction firm needs to pre-booking to purchase this kind of the best quality of constructoin material from overseas before three worths. So, it must not have enough time to pre-booking to purchase this kind of best quality of constructoin materials when they are used rapaidly within one month, due to this one month is the final finishing time to this construction firm within one month. Hence, limited construction material supply number and limited finishing time to build this new 40 floors house within this final one month .

So , not proficient construction workers number , limit number of construction material and per day 8 hours which is its limited resources in behavioral eocnomy view. Moreover, total 50 proficient and not proficient 50 construction workers (human resource employees number) will cause this constructoin firm , it will possible need to build this new 40 floors house are more than one month, if these 50 proficient construction workers , they have more than 30 at least number, they are absent to cause their overall construction workers' efficiency to be fallen down, due to the other 50 not proficient constuction numbers must need their teaching how to cooperate ad how use less materials to build this new 40 floor hourse rapidly in order to raise overall constructon team efficiency and avoid to delay more than one month time to build this 40 floors new house successfully within this final one month time.

Hence, it explains that when one organization has more employees, it does not represent that this organization must need to use more resource to achieve its any mission, such as this construction firm case, although it has 50 not proficient construction workers, they need to use more construction materials to build this new 40 floors house in this construction site (A). But, in fact, it has other 50 proficient construction workers, they know how to reduce construction materials to build every building floor wall for this new 40 floors building house. So, they can teach the not proficient building workers to know hoe to avoid to use extra excess constructon material to finish to construct every building fllor wall. SO, although, it has 50 not proficient construction workers number, but they can be taught to learn how to reduce to use these limited the best quality of construction materials to build this 40 floors new house. It implies that if the construction workers number can increase, e.g. increases more 50 not proficient construction workers, this the best quality of construction material resource number must not need to increase demand, because this construction site (A) has 50 proficient construction workers , they can teach these 50 not proficient construction workers how to avoid to use extra excess this kind of high quality construction material to build this new 40 floor house efficiently and effectively within this one month.

Hence, if this construction firm won't have more than 30 proficient workers number is absent in this final one month, it will have enough proficient construction workers to teach these 50 not proficient construction workers to know how to use this high quality of construction materials to build this 40 floors new house building in order to avoid waste or construction material need shortage challenge occurs in this final one month time.

Consequently , it ought finish to build this 40 floors new house building within this month. Hence, it explains why its this kind of high quality of construction material resource need must not increase, because if its all proficient construction workers is absent and their absent number is less than 30, then they have enough proficient construction workers number , they can teach this 50 not proficient construction workers how to avoid to use extra excess construction materials resource number in order to have enough construction material resource supply to satisfy this new 40 floors building house to finish construction within one month finishing date need.

On conclusion, in organizational behavioral economic view, it explains that resource use need must not be influenced to increase when the organization's employees number increase. It depends on whether the organization has how many talent and proficient workers number in order to assist them and teach the not proficient employees how to use resource to manufacture any kinds of products in order to avoid to spend extra excess of resource need. Hence, organizational behavioral economic view, it can explain that any organization's increase to employees number, it does not mean that its resource number is also needed to increase. Moreover, in organizational behavioral economic view, it also explains that if the organization can have many proficient workers to help it to do any complex tasks, they will help it to bring avoiding waste or excess extra resource to use advantage, because they ought know whether how they work, they can help the organization to improve performance or raise efficiency e.g. car manufacture, computer manufacture, television manufcture etc. home electronic products or car leisure products. Due to that manufacturre processes are complex, if the organization can have more proficient high skillful workers to help it to manufacture their products. They ought help it to use lesser manufacturing time and less manufacturing resource to finish any above these products to compare not proficient or low skillful manufacture workers. So, in long time, the organization must may earn economic low cost benefits from proficient worker individual high manufacturing skillful knowledge behavior or performance. So, organizational behavioral economic theory explains why even the organization plans to increase employees number, it's resources number won't be influenced to increase rapidly because when the organization's proficient high skillful workers number is more 2 times at least than not proficient low skillful workers number. They ought have enough effort to train and teach and cooperate with the not proficient low skillful manufacture workers to improve their manufacture skills in order to raise manufacturing efficiency and reduce extra excess resources waste and avoid to bring long term resource waste economic loss.

So, any manufacturing organizations must need to increase proficient workers number to assist the not proficient low skillful workers to learn how to improve their skills and know how to reduce to use excess resources to keep to manufacture the highest number of products aim frequently. Consequently, the organization will bring long term low resource use manufacturing economic benefit.

What factors influence student makes subject choice decision
Behavioral economic on law and economy subject choice how to student individual subject learning choice behavior in universities economy and law subjects choice example, whether students will make subject either law or economt subject choice, it depends on future lawyer and economist salary whether which occupation can earn long term more salary comparision in order to decide wither law or economy degree learn.

Some university students make these two subjects either one learning choice, they will decide whether school fee is how much more than future salary earns, or personal interest psychological factor influences. So, if the student feels more interest to learn law degree , then he won't choose economy degree between these two degrees. Behavioral economy theory can be applied to explain this student individual economy and law degrees choice behavior because his subject choice decision is depended on personal psychological interest factor more than school fee or future salary possible earn economic salary reward factor influences. But, I assume that if the university can give scholorship for economic and law degree student when the student feels the law degree scholarship higher than economic degree. Then, he will decide to choose law degree to study more than economy degree. He chooses to study law degree because he hopes to earn higher scholarship.

IN behavioral economy principle , it can be applied to explain this student degree choice behavior. However, applying behavioral economy view, it assumes these principles to analyze whether how the student chooses to study the degree. The principles or factors may influence his degree choice may include: Cost and benevits, e.g. the student fee and future salary for the degree, when the student has interest to study law and economic degree. So, he needs to do degree choice. Then, he may compare whether how much law and economy degree school fee, it may be possible future earn salary, scholarship possible reward. All of these factors concern the price for law and economy degree (external cost) and future possible income (salary) for economist and lawyer occupation. It is behavioral law and economic factor to influence how the student chooses either law or economic degree to study in the university.

For example, when the (A) university on student enrolls to the (A) university before, he needs to choose wither law or economy degree to study. I assume that he only feels interest to study these two degrees. Then, he will compare school fees, if law degree school fee is per year US$5,000, 4 years is US$20,000 and economy degree school fee is per year US$3,000, 4 years is US$12,000. Although, it seems that economy 4 year school fee is more less US$8,000 to compare law degree 4 year, but this student also compare possible future salary for lawyer and economist occupation. He believes that future lawyer salary may pay more 4 times to compare economists salary after 5 years working experience. Although, if this student chooses economy degree to study, he may have chance to earn scholarship if his examination can be good, but it is one time short time economic researd and this scholarship reward is not sure that he must earn, if he can not get at least 5 (A) grade any one economic subject papers in this university cconomy degree structure. Otherwise, if he chooses to study law and get 5 (A) grade any one law subject papers in the university law degree structure, he can not get scholarship for this law degree. hence , he makes final choice to study law degree, although he can not get scholarship and school fee is more than economy degree. But he believes that he can earn higher salary when he can be one lawyer and he works after 5 years, his salary may be paid more than one economist salary.

In behavioral economic view, it can be applied to explain this university student his degree choice behavior, then he has interest to study law and economy degree. He must need to make one degree choice to graduate, then he may make degree choice decision by external economic cost (degree price) and future reward (possible income) behavioral economic factor . Then, he can judge whether which degree is more suitable to choose to study in this university.

How organization improvement may bring economic benefits

Can organizational economies, e.g. transaction cost economics, agency theory, organizational theory , e.g. models of formal organizational independent of the strategies, improve organizational behavior in order to bring economic benefit, e.g. development potentially valuable resources and capabilities, it can raise internal organizatonal strengths and avoid weaknesses in SWOT strategy in order to imporve performance and bring organizational internal economic benefit in organizational behavioral economic view.

For manufacturing industry example, if the car manufacturers can attempt to discover the most efficient steel, or different kinds of car components material, but they can help it to manufacture many high quality cars. Then, their manufactury cost reduce , but its any model of car quality does not caused to poor. Then, this car firm can apply the most efficient and the most high component materials to help it to manufacture high quality cars.

Although, it must need to spend time to research how to invest the most efficient and high quality car manufacture components, but if it can apply the most efficient and the high quality components to help it to manufacture any new model of cars. Then, new components research spending time can bring long term low manufacturing cost and high quality of cars to achieve long time economic benefits.

So, on behavioral economic view, organization's spending time on different kind of cheap and high quality car manufacture manufacture components research and research expenditure spending on new kinds of different car manufacture components, it can help it to sell the high quality of different model of cars to satisfy car buyer comfortable needs. Moreover, it can earn high profit, when it 's any car manufacture component cost reduces. So, SWOT internal strengths (high quality and low cost) to this car manufacturer. It may help it to bring long term raising profit economic benefit, when its any new model of car prices do not need raise, but their compared material manufacture cost reduce, due to new kinds of car manufacture component materials can be invented in success.

Hence, high quality and low cost of car manufacture component invention researching on spending time and research experiment expenditure is value to this car manufacture company, because if high quality and low cost car manufacture component experience succeeds, it can help it to improve any new model of cars quality , but the most important factor is that its any new model of cars prices do not need increase. So, car buyer individual purchase desire won't be influenced to choose any brand of car seller to replace it more easily.

For one drug development process, case example ,I assume that this drug manufacture firm can attempt to spend 10 years time, but it can help it has possible to help it to invent one kind of new pharmaceutical drugs to kill cancer cells for global cancer patients. So, its spending time research on new drugs to kill any kinds of cancers cellers and experimentation expenditure is value, because it can help it to bring economic benefit when global will have many cancer patients believe its new discovery of cancer drugs , it may help them to kill cancer cells to get health or reduce death chance ratio raises after 10 years.

Consequently, in soon future, it's global cancer patients number may increase when they choose to buy its future new cancer drugs paroduct. It may bring high profit economic benefit. So, on organizational behavioral economic view, when the organization spends long time and experimentation expenditure to research new resources, if these new resources can be invcntcd in success and it ensures help it to increase clients number to order to bring future economic benefit. The organization is value to spend time and expenditure to carry on new resources research.

● Can organization apply behavioral economic demand to evaluate work performance for whole different departments?

Behavioral economies investigation may include evaluating demand for a commodity (such as drug experimentation and car manufacturing component material etc.) is given changes in price, using hypothetical purchase tasks, which are a reliable and efficient assessment method. Can behavior management examine work performance evaluation? The work performance evaluation target includes that employee individual and different department will performance evaluation in organization.

I believe high quality or low quality training , which can be evaluated whether the employee individual work performance or the department overall employees work performance can be improved after training. So, if the department employee individual or all employers work performance can be improved, e.g. work efficiency raises, client satisfactory feeling raises, product sale number . Then, the training is a high quality training to help the organization to earn future high economic benefit. Otherwise , if the organization can not earn above any one good result. Then, the training ia a low quality training.So, any organization can attempt to observe any department overall performance and employee individual performance in order to evaluate whether it can provide high or low quality of training to let employees to learn.

So, employee individual behavior can bring performance evidence to let the organization to evaluate whether its training is useful or not useful to achieve its training aim, e.g. when the car manufacturer provides money, time, effort training arrangement to teach all workers to learn how to manufacture car skill. After training provision, many of them, they do not need to work over time more than one hour to manufacture daily of least 10 cars per employee.Before, any one worker must need to spend more than one hour over time to manufacture daily 10 more cars.

So, when this car manufacture skillful improvement train is provided more than one hour more than one hour , none of them, they need work over time in order to manufacture more than at least 10 cars number per day. It seems that training improvement arrangement can be used to evaluate whether employee individual efficiency can be raised in organizational behavioral economic view.

Hence, any organization's internal training provision knowledge resource, it can be evaluated employees' behavioral performance can be improved, about being available to work, about role performance . It assumes that employees are likely to come to work and remain in the organization if they obtain satisfaction from their jobs, and that they are likely to put use effort and work more effectively if they are to be reward more for their effort and performance can be comfirmed to improved by management after they are taught by training. So, when the employee hopes to raise salary, he must hard to learn any new knowledge from the organizational training. Then, training can help the " expectation good reward employees" can improve performance in organizational behavioral economic view.

It is one important successful factor to help the organization to innovate and bring economic benefit, when the organization can implement any new useful training to improve any new useful training to imprve empllyee skills. It means that training is one long term economic organizational strategy, it depends on whether the training is useful or is ot useful in order to help any old employees to raise or improve their skills to achieve raising efficiency and satisfactory client service , sale product number, product manufacture increasing number aims.

● How organizational ethic influence employee behavior ?
Organizational ethic behavior concerns with explaining employee individual behavior in organization, e.g. ethical decision making, ethical conduct for example, when one marketing department manager does not attempt to carrying on any data research about new market research to sell the new model iphone to any country. He only depends on his personal judgement, he believes that this new invention of US iphone producs, they ought to be sell to Korean new iphone market, because he feels Korean must

prefer to choose to buy US drand of new iphone products to compare other countries iphone product. However, this iphone marketing development manager lacks enough data research for different Korean iphone buyer age target, purchase experience, purchase desire to conclude Korean iphone buyers must like to buy any brand of US iphone products in preference.

His non ethical new iphone invention decision making to choice Korean ipohone buyers market will bring time waste rick to satisfy Korean iphone buyers' needs to replace other new model ipone users market, e.g. Hong KOng, China, ipone market. So, his ethical decision making to Korean iphone buyers ne iphone invention market may bring less economic benefit to this US iphone manufacture firm. So, this new model ipohone marketing development immoral judgement of this iphone marketing development manager individual decision making to Korean new model ipone invention to Korean ipone users, it can bring high economic loss to this US iphone firm.Otherwise, if this marketing department manager can spend time to carry on data gathering to make more accurate new model iphone invention decision making to choose which one country, then his ethical decision making may help his this US iphone firm to reduce new iphone invention loss risk. So, it explains that why ethic organizational behavior may influence the firm can earn more or less economic benefit. SO, ethic or moral behavior can influence the organization can earn how much economic benefit in long term significantly in organizational behavioral economic view.

● Can improve energy efficiency by organization building occupant's energy consumption relative behavior to bring economic benefit?
Reducing energy consumption in building , it must improve efficiency by building, but whether they have close cause and effect relationship between occupant's energy consumption behavior and improvement energy efficiency to the building? IN fact, high efficiency equipment is being developed, it can help any building to save energy and economic effectiveness, if building energy is subject to uncertainties, such as whether variations, human operations, human behavior changes and government policies. So, building technology equipment improvement may be one main factor to help buildings to save energy . But why occupant behavior may help building to save energy by their daily energy consumption behavior. The occupant energy behavioral user inputs factor may include: Weather

influences, internal heat gain, efficiencies, simplied/ normal occupant behaviors, e.g. a high efficiency chiller can save very limited energy in cold climates due to minimal cooling load, and a good designed natural ventilation building won't work if the occupants do not open windows when outdoor air favors cooling. So, it seems that if one living building hopes to reduce energy consumption, instead of building equipment technological change , e.g. air condition facilities, building occupants , artificial intelligent light, life, their daily energy consumption behaviors, they can influence the living building's energy consumption level in occupant energy consumption behavior and building energy saving economic benefit view.

In fact, when the occupant considers hot water, air condition, energy gas electricity expenditure, he won't use excess electricity, gas resources, because he needs to pay more energy expenditure , when gas and electricity energy consumption expenditure is applied to any business organization offices, warehouses , shops working facilities environment, such as offices, warehouses , shops can often use less electricity, gas energy far ther employees daily work . In long time, the organization must may reduce much electricity, gas energy expenditure for whole organizations business activities. In organizational behavior economic view, organizational energy consumption reduces it can help it to bring less expenditure spending economic benefit.

● Can Amazon e-commerce organization business activities bring economic benefit to global societies?

Amazon e-commerce is one online product sale e-commerce organization. Any one country e-buyer can use his/her home computer to click to Amazon webstores, when he/she saw the product phone and price, then he/she feels the product's price is reasonable and he/she believes that he/she can make the best choice to buy the product. Then, he/she can pay visa to buy the product from Amazon webstore.
Amazon can bring the most convenient online sale channel to global any one e-buyer. The e-buyer can buy the oveseas product from its e-webstores . He does not need to catch air plane to fly to the e-sellers' shop. he can pay visa to pay the product from Amazon e-webstores any time immediately. All Amazon e-webstores . He can open 24 hours, so all webstores have no close

time. So , it can bring busy working people, they do not need to spend long time to visit any shops to make purchase decision. For busy working people example, time has important value to them, they do not want to waste time to make any purchase choice.

So, Amazon gives " economic purchase time benefit " to global any one full time working people. In their psychology, Amazon can help them to save much time to go to onlinc shopping purchase chance at homes. They can stay at homes to shopping. Even, when they give their their address to Amazon to know, Amazon will deliver their products to their homes within several days rapidly. Also , they do not need to pay money to buy its products immediately. They can only pay visa to buy the product from Amazon webstores. So, they can save " consumption money" to use for another need in short time. So, one individual e-air ticket buyer, Amazon can bring economic benefit to him, he does not need to buy air ticket to fly to another country to buy the product. Amazon webstores are given more different kinds of similar brand products to let him to choose in order to pay the most reasonable price, working people do not need to spend much visiting shop time to choose any products in order to make the final purchase decision at home rapidly, any one has visa card , he/she can buy the product from Amazon webstores at homes.

Instead of individual e-buyer ecommerce time benefit, spending little time product choice, reducing catching air plane to visit another country seller shop to pay air ticket expense and travelling time spending activities to every e-buyer . Amazon also brings global economic benefits to any one country. When the e-buyer lives in one country to buy the product, it is saved in the overseas country's warehouse. Then, the product must need to deliver to his home by air plane. So, all of Amazon products can bring global goods air transport delivering service to any one overseas buyer, when the product is saved in the overseas seller's warehouse. Any one Amazon product overseas transpor delivery service activity, it can help air goods transport service need increases as well as their goods air transport service income will also increase. Amazon can bring global air goods transport service need increases. It can assist global GDP air goods transport industry grows, and economic benefit for the country's air plan goods delivery service industry development in long term. Hence, on behavioral economic view, Amazon online sale channel ,it can help global economic benefit to air plane goods delviery service industy as well as individual differeent country e-buyer individual time saving and short term money saving economic benefit by visa payment method.

Moreover, Amazon alsoo creates more high technology employment chance to any one country because Amazon owns many offices and warehouses in different countries, due to it is one high technological e-commerce online sale organization, It must need many high skillful website designers to help it to design different countries webstores in order to satisfy any one e-buyer online purchase need. So, it creates high technology job chance to any one country webstore designers . It can help them to raise competitive effort when any one graduate pursues website designer career. IN Amazon provides good employent chance for any one country computer ecommerce designers in order to let them to earn high salary. Also, Amazon public e-commerce organization provides good chance for any one country author to earn royalty income when he/she publishes any electronic or paper books to sell from Amazon publish. It gives good writing skillful authors have more writing chance to help them to sell electronic books and /or paper books' from its different countries webbook stores to different countries' readers in short time. It can help them to increase book sale chance to let different countries book buyers can know whether new book topic to the author, he/she will publish soon. So, it brings author's new writing mind training chance when he/she needs to compare book sale rank from Amazon webstores.

Hence, Amazon can bring social employment benefit and author individual skillful training advantage and royalty income benefit to any on country author in nowadays online published industty. So, Amazon online business activities can increase global social employment chance, encourages global authors attempt to train writing skill, helps e-buyers to save visiting shops shopping time and air ticket expenditure for global overseas buyers.

● How and why Amazon e-commerce organization influence global consumee behavioral changes to bring ecommerce benefits to sellers?

In behavioral economic view, Amazon changes consumers behavior as well as product sellers sale method, such as global consumer sellers began to accept online purchase method to replace frequent visiting shop purchase method and global sellers began to accept to apply Amazon webstores to help them to sell products from its online sale channel to replace opening shops locate to the country sale channel.

The advantages to global sellers may include they do not need to pay rent or buy the shops, they can use Amazon webstores to show their different kinds of products photos and prices to let any one online buyer to know . The advantage to global buyers, they do not need to spend time to visit any countries shops to choose products in order to make purchase decision. They only need to spend some time to visit amazon any one country's webstore to see any brands of product photos and know their prices to different kinds of products to compare design and price and functions among of them in the online visiting short time when they stay at home to trun on themselves home computers . So, future home consumption behavior may replace visiting shop consumption behavior. Amazon 's online purchase method will encourage global many sellers have began to believe traditional visiting shop purchase model can not be accepted to global any one consumer more easily, when any one owns computer and internet service at home in common. Then, global shops number will reduce, due to different kinds of product websites purchase model needs number increases to global product sellers, they will close their shops and open themselves webstores or choose Amazon webstore to help them to sell their products conveniently. Consequently, global online purchase and sale transactions number will be influenced to increase by e-commerce organization development.

● Have they close relationship between consumer behavioral change and economic change?

● How does consumer behavioral change impact economic change?

● How does consumer behavior bring positive or negative influence to economic growth or economic recession to the country?

I shall attempt to apply behavioral economic theory to explain their cause and effect relationship why and hoe global economy growth or recession may be impacted by global consumer behavior change reasons ae below:

I shall indicate travellingleisure and goods air plane transport industries example, since air planes are invented, it is a kind rapid air transport tool, it can help human to do both kinds of transport asrvice, one is goods transport and another is human transport . So, any individual or business goods can be delivered to another country offices or homes by air planes transport tools rapidly. SO, air planes can create more overseas purchase and sale business activities chance between different countries nowadays. Moreover, internet invention, it also increase more e-coomerce online purchase and sale business acitivies to global any one online buyer, he/she only needs to apply computer tool to click to the online seller webstore, when he /she likes the product, he/she can pay visa to buy the product from the onlin seller webstore at home conveniently.

Hence, e-commerce encourages global consumers to choose to buy any products from internet channel, it also brings global goods are needed to transport by air planes between different countries, e.g. one US online buyer makes purchase decision from onlin channel, then he chooses the product from Korean one online seller webstore. After he pays visa to the Korean online seller webstore , then the Korea seller will follow his US address to send the product to the US buyer's home after several days rapidly.

Hence, it explains that if future global consumers like to buy any products from any one country's onine sell webstore. Then, the product must need to be delivered to the online buyer's home. When the seller's product is not located to the online buyer's country warehouse. It needs to be delivered by air plane. When, global there are man consumers, their traditional visiting shops purchase habits are influenced to change online visiting webstores habits. Then, when their purchase habits are influenced to change by rapid, convenient, visa card payment online purchase method at home, time online purchase technological new payment channel method.

In future new online purchase trend development, it may influence future global traditional visiting shops consumption model to change visiting webstores consumption model. Consequently, consumers will choose to pay visa online purchase at home in preference. Also, it encourages visa card purchase , consequently, online purchase may influence these industries development, airlines goods transport service needs increase, it can increase new visa cards number to the frequent online channel e-buyer number. So, online consumption encourages global households save long time money in banks, because we can pay money by visa card payment after we buy any products from online. Global bank may have more money to save longer time from global households, long time money save , because we do not need to withdraw money to buy any expensive products, immediately, e.g. computer , television, furniture etc. When global households begin to accept online purchase method is better to compare visiting shop purchase method. So, future global airline goods transport and bank saving businesses these two industries may have positive impact by future global online buyers raising number.

Hence, when global consumers behaviors began to change online purchase , their online purchase activities may influence global banks can have long time saving money and airlines goods transport need increase rapidly. However, online purcahse activies will bring negative consumers emotion impact to some businesses, e.g. property rent business, because when the country has high population of consumers, they choose online purchases, they won't often vitis shops to choose any kind of products frequently, they only like to stay at home and turn on themselves home computers to find whether global whom sellers, they have webstores to let global consumers to buy their products from online channel. Due to the cuntry willl not have many consumers like to spend time to visit any shops in the country. It means that the country will have many shops are needed to be close, because there are less number peple visit the businessmen shops every day. It will cause property rent service providers can not increase rent income, even decrease rent income, when there are many businessmen close their shops and change onine webstores to replace actual shops. Hence, it seems that online buyers number increases, it may also brings positive impact to influence shop rent service income decreases to the property rent developers.

On global macro economic changing environment, online buyers number increases, it can encourage any kinds of products, they can sell more more easily. So, global product sale number may be influenced to increase rapidly, when global online purchase and sale transactions number increase, GDP on any kinds of product income may be influenced to increase . So, online buyers number increases, it must may bring positive impact to influence global trading GDP high growth, but global shops rent income property developers may be influenced to reduce, due to there are many shops may be caused to close in possible.

How travellers' leisure need change, it may influence travelling leisure service industry development? I shall attempt to explain how COVID 19 disease influences global travellers lesiure need change and airpine and travelling service providers, e.g. hotels, travelling agents, their leisure service needs change. Nowadys, COVID 19 disease has caused global many travellers feel fear to catch airplanes, because air planes all windows are needed to close, he/she has COVID disease, then he/she can bring any one passegner to get this kind of disease by air plane close window air environment. So, when globa many travellers feel afreaid to catch air planes, this kind of COVID 9 air contact disease, it can cause global travellers number has began to reduce, many of travelles began to reduce travelling times per year, even 0 time travel per year. Consequently, it will bring negative impact to global travelling industry development.

Firstly, COVID 19 disease influences global traveller individual travelling desire decreases, every traveller began to avoid to catch air planes to travel. So, any country;s airlines air planes flying times began to reduce, because it is no full seats booking to any airlinees. It means that airlinee must decrease income, alsoo they need to pay parking airplanes rent to any countries airports. So, fixed rent expenditure will need to pay, and many airlines began to dismiss the excess extra number of airline front service staffs, e.g. airport front service staffs, air plane check in /out staffs, even pilots number began also decreased.

So, airline unemployment ratio increases , it causes pilots, airlines service staffs need to change jobsm even some coutnries pilots , choose to do simple goods delivery jobs in supermarkets or securities. Also, COVID 19 disease influences hotels, travelling agents income began to reduce, because there are none many travellers need to live hotels, and they do not need travelling agents to help them to arrange any travelling journeys. So , COVID 19 disease influences many different countries travellers began choose any leisure activities to replace travel, because they feel afraid to get COVID 19 disease when they need to sit in closed window air plane environment.

This kind of disease can influence any one travller individual leisure choice began to change, such as they began to forgive travel siure activities, they will spend holiday to do other leisure activities in themselves countries , e.g. climbing mountain, swimming, running, playing table tennis, tennis etc. different outdoor sports. all of these leisure sports have same features, global any one leisure needer, he does not catch air plane to fo to another country to carry on playing these any one sport and he/she does not need to pay more price to enjoy these sports. Otherwise m travelling leisure activity, it must need any one leisure needer to spend much expenditure to enjoy this kind of leisure activity . So, it explains why many travellers beagan to choose to do any kinds of sports to replace spending money to enjoy travel leisure in their holidays,

On conclusion,this COVID 19 disease had influenced global travel leisure businesses and travel related leisure service industries income and travellers number began to reduce and any countries GDP on travelling industry will have negative economic recession occurrence in this COVID 19 disease global envionment. Hence, it implies thaat consumers (travellers) behavior leisure activities need, it may influence global business activities increase or decrease , global economic growth or recession, they have close cause and effect relationship between consumer behavioral change and industries GDP changes in behavioral economic view.

● Can economic environment influence individual learning performance ?

Why does student enrollment rise when the economy recession? When a struggling economy certainly forces extra pressure on young students seeking funds for loans and tuition cost, the enrollment rates for colleges continuous to rise. In fact, some experts theoritize that a poor economy environment actually helps a stimulate student enrollment. Whether it is the economy , new academic programs or better recruiting, community colleges are seeing an enrollment boom, when enrollment has been growing steadily , it may increase year institutions. To help prospective student interests when providing all current students with diverse support.

What the motivation had factors that are encouraging students to enroll, e.g. whether it is that the country 's young people feel the country begins have poor economy, so many of them choose to enroll schools to learn new knowledge, because scoial poor economy environment, it won't have many employers like to pay more salaries to employ new employees, consequencey, unemployment rate will rise, it causes students feel difficult to find jobs to do in general, even graduate students. So, it seems that economy recession may encourage students further study, because job supply is decreasing. so, it causes many young people choose to spend time to further study in order to wait economy recovery later. Then, they can prepare to seek any new jobs more easily when there are many employers like to increase employees number.

So, it explains that they have case and effect relationship between student enrollment number and the country's economy growth or recession or recovery, For example, when the country economy growth, in society, it will have many employers like to spend more salaries to employ new employees, because there are many people like to consume, when most of them have jobs to do and earn higher income. so, it seems that in society consumer individual increasing consumption attitude/desire that can help businesses grow, when businesses have more customers, they have effort to pay money to buy any things to use.

Businessmen ought need to increase employees number to help them to develop themselve businesses more successfully. So, it is economy growth period, moreover, many young people feel economy growth can create more employment chance in society. So, it encourages many students choose to forget to continue to pursue high level academic education, e.g. when the student had graduated undergraduate degree, due to he feels social economic environment is improved. So, employers are seeking new employees to help them to develop businesses. So, employment chance increases and salaries level will also rise. So, it encourages many undergraduate students do not want to pursue master degree. Because they believe that they can find jobs to do more easily in this time. So, it seems that the society's present economy suitation is either goos or worse, it can impact students to choose continue pursue higher learning stage or not. So, it explains that student individual learning desire and the social economy have close influential relationship.

What factors influence consumer purchase decision ?

Economic theory is based on the assumption that investors and consumers are rational and very efficient machines. They make the best choices for themselves. Laboratory tests reveal that investors' behaviors are much more complicated relative to the behavior assumes in most economic theories. Hence, economic theories is used by economists, they try to explain economic phenomena, to interpret why and how the economy behaves and what is the best to solution, how to influence or solve these economic phenomean. In principle, the approach to economic theory is divided into positive and normative.

The most popular economic theories include; Analyses of different market structures have yields economic theories that dominate the study of microeconomics. IN general, economic theory is applied to market organizations. They are perfect competition, monololistic competition, olgopolu, imperfect competition.

So, in any business environment, business on abve four type of economic organizations, they may attempt to apply economic theory to complex consumers behavior. Consumer behavior theory is the study of have people make decisions when they purchase, helping businesses and marketers capitalise on these behaviors by predicting how and when a consumer will make a purchase in economic environment organizational view.

In fact, in societies any economic factors may influence consumer behavior. Economic factors that influence consumer behaviors are : personal income, family income, income expectation, savings, liquid asset of consumer. So, it seems that personal income of a person is determinant of consumer individual buying behavior.

Hence, the role theory says that much of what we buy is to fulfill to characteristics of a role we see ourselves as playing. This can help us understand consumer behavior because people are more likely to buy things for what they mean not for what they do. So, the theory is consumer realistic because of consumers focus on a modest let of important goods and services, they may able to achieve societies is close to the theoretical optimum in term over utility.

● How economic theory explains our social consumer behavior causes?
For example, one product brand and advertisement strategy, if the product can develop good attractive advertisement and famous brand. Its campaigns may be a real asset in economic view to better meet the needs of its customers and increases sales (socio-economic classification).

If act, instead of economic factor can influence consumer behavior, other factors may also influence they include psychological, social , cultural personal factors, e.g. social class, role and status, personal age, occupation, life style, personality, motivation, past purchase experience. All of these are the consumer individual psychological factor. So, economic environment changes, it may influence consumers, how to decide to buy the kind of products, but this economic factor, it can not control or derminate overall consumer behavior in the overall consumption mrket (country) , in maco economic vie , the micro economic view, psychology factor to the consumer, it can also dominate or control the consumer behavior, e.g. product choice. For example, one lawyer, he had good lawyer job and high income to support him to pay one time expenditure to buy a new car, so he does not pay instalement to the car seller to buy the new car. So, in behavioral economic view, he won't have economic pressure to buy the new car, he does not need to pay installment and interest to own the new car after one year. Hence, when he gathers information concerns the new car technology development, he spends time to compare the new car different brands, price new car dealr choice, purchase timing and amount, after purchase repair service behavior. He makes the evaluation of alternative to different brands of new cars. Although, brand (A) is new car, its price is more expensive to compare other kinds of cars, because it has good design, large size, more seats, steel quality for driving safety reasons. He has enough money economic effort to choose to buy this brand (A) new car. But, when he compares it to another brand (B) new car. Although, its present car price is cheaper, but it does not represent tht its stell quality is worse, or not more driving safety and he also knows that the brand (B) new car will have another new car model to promote to car market, after three months. Moreover, brand (B) new car seller can build famous car brand image to same to brand (A) new car by its advertisement channel.

Hence, it seems that it is one perfect competition (fair competition) new car market in this country. Any new car sallers can dominate or control their new car sale price freely. So, this country new car market competition is serious, because this high income lawyer spends time to compare the both brand (A) and (B) new cars. He will be influenced to choose to buy brand (B) new car by its advertisement. So, this lawyer car purchaser will not feel that friends believe him have high income to influence him to choose to buy the brand (A) new car. He only consider whether which brand (A) and (B) nee car price is more reasonable factor to influence him to make the final new car purchase decision. So, the brand (B) new car's advertisement had persuaded him to choose to buy (A) last invention new car after 3 months. He chooses to delay time to buy brand (B) 's new invention car after 3 months, because he does not need to drive one new car immediately.

Hence, it seems that economic theory factor won't be the main factor to influence the lawyer to buy the brand (A) new car immediately, althought he has high stable income job. His psychological factor also influences his new car brand choice decision, e.g. he will feel that whether it can represent he has high social status or class when friends know he had owned one high pricc of ncw car, whether a high price of new car must represent he has high income of lawyer occupation, so, it seems that this high income lawyer must not choose to buy the high price of new car. he must neeed time to gather or research information to evaluate whether which brand of new car is valid to choose to buy.

Consequently, economic theory must not explain absolute right consumer behavior, it also depends on other factor, e.g. behavioral economic psychological factor, to assist it to conclude more accurate judgement why and how the consumer does his/her final purchase decision. So, psychologic economic theory can apply psychology and economic theory to conclude more clear understanding how and why the consumer chooses to do his/her final purchase decision in nowadays consumption market.

Whether what are the actual benefits , they may bring to influence our societies change better? I shall attempt to to explain above question. Economic is the social science that examines how individuals, businesses and entire societies manage scarce resources. Resources are by nature , limited. Only a finite amount of land exists, e.g. and people do not have unlimieted time to meet all of their needs and wants. So, if we can learn ho to apply behavioral economy theory to avoid resources waste, then our societies ought develop better.

Our society had changed from traditional economy to develop to nowadays knowledge economy. Traditional economy only produce and take what they need, so there is no waste or inefficiencies involved in produdig the goods required to survive as a society. However, traditional economy also have disadvantages, such as it isolates the people within that economt, large outside economies can win a traditional economy. It offers choices, these may be a lower overall quality of life, it creates specific health risk, unpredictability creates survival uncertainties.

Although, our societies had been experiencing knowledge economy, but it also have disadvantage, knowledge economy means that our societies or business organizations need to learn how ro use knowledge management to keep business growth or social developing. Knowledge management is a systematic approach to capturing and making use of a organization collective expertise to create value. The potential advantages of effective knowledge management are significant , but as with most processes, advantages of knowledge management or knowledge ecnmic society may include:

Improved organizational or social productivities better and faster decision making, quicker problem solving, increased rate of innovation, supported employee/citizen growth and development within organizations or societies, sharing of specialiat expertise, better communication, improved business processes.

Hence if the organization or society can apply behavioral economic theory to learn knowledge management system , it can help the organization or society to develop better or more easier, e.g. create better products and services , develop better strategies, improve profitability or productivity, reuse existing skills and expertise, increase operational efficiency and staff productivity, recognise market trends early and gain on advantage over rivals make the most of organizations or social intellectual capital . Hence, it explains why when our organizations or societies can apply behavioral economy theory to learn how to apply knowledge management system to develop our organiztations or societies. Then, our societies or organizations will avoid to waste social resource organizational resource as well as achieve more productivities or service improvement, even gain profitability, it is the final aim of why our organizations or / and societies need to attempt to learn how to apply knowledge management system to achieve any objectives in behavioral economy view.

On conclusion, behavioral economic is the study of the effect that our societiesand organizations need to learn how psychological factors have on the economic decision making process of individuals. The importance of understanding behavioral economics for marketers is immeasurable as it follows for a better understanding of the human mind. So, behavioral economics plays a important role in our live and in the eocnomy. It helps governments and businesses learn on every day consumers activities and explains why we consume goods and services , the way we do, why we make certain choices, about ourselves or others and how we decide of action . Hence, behavioral economists need to examine each of these day -to -day choice resulting in progressive understanding of human behavior that combines both psychology and economy.

How do rules influence economic behavior?
Why are the rules of the economic system important? In our societies , our economic behavior occurs in a climate of formal and informal rules. There sulres often act as incentives and influenced the choices people make, people choose to do jobs taht do not keep them fit, and now they have to make more time to stay healthy. So, our societies are experiencing behavioral economic rules made in order to let every one need to adapt how to change and influence to our lives. it is one actual knowledge economic society or knowledge economic social living mode that we need to learn how to adapt to live. We need to learn how to apply knowledge of economic changing behavior. UNderstanding behavioral economic and psychology for social impact our businesses can bring products , sale growth more easily or our societies can be improved to our living quality better.

The relationship between behavioral economy and our society , it may explain that if the result of economic scarcity in a society occurrence, due to that productive resources are limited, therefore, people can not have all the goods and services, they want, a result, they must choose some things and give up others , like individuals, governments and societies , experience scarcity because human wats exceed with can be made from all available resources.

Behavioral economic is the study of psychology as it relates to the economic decision making processes of individuals and organizations. Behavioral economy theory uses psychological experimentation to develop theories about human decision making and has identified a range of biases as a result of the way people think and feel. BE is trying to change the way economists think about people's perception of value and expressed preferences.

However, in our societies, we need have three basic economic problems. Economic systems is as a type social system must confront and solve the three quantities of goods shall be produced, how much and which of alternative tools and services shall be produced, how shall goods be produced what technology a well as for whom are the goods , or services produced who benefts?

All of these are our daily economic problems any organizations (societies) had been changing. We need new social science behavioral economy theory to help use to solve any one of social economic individual problems, for example, when a particular incident becomes cognitively available, it is became of social influence. Individuals are specially averse to losses, but how do we know whether we are facing a loss or instead of a foregone gain ? What is the status from which losses are measured ? how might social influence reduces or increase people's willingness to sacrifice their material sale-interest for the sake of fairness?

...

CHAPTER THREE

How organizational outsourcing improve performance

Can organizational economies, e.g. transaction cost economics, agency theory, organizational theory , e.g. models of formal organizational independent of the strategies, improve organizational behavior in order to bring economic benefit, e.g. development potentially valuable resources and capabilities, it can raise internal organizatonal strengths and avoid weaknesses in SWOT strategy in order to imporve performance and bring organizational internal economic benefit in organizational behavioral economic view.

For manufacturing industry example, if the car manufacturers can attempt to discover the most efficient steel, or different kinds of car components material, but they can help it to manufacture many high quality cars. Then, their manufactury cost reduce , but its any model of car quality does not caused to poor. Then, this car firm can apply the most efficient and the most high component materials to help it to manufacture high quality cars. Although, it must need to spend time to research how to invest the most efficient and high quality car manufacture components, but if it can apply the most efficient and the high quality components to help it to manufacture any new model of cars. Then, new components research spending time can bring long term low manufacturing cost and high quality of cars to achieve long time economic benefits.

So, on behavioral economic view, organization's spending time on different kind of cheap and high quality car manufacture manufacture components research and research expenditure spending on new kinds of different car manufacture components, it can help it to sell the high quality of different model of cars to satisfy car buyer comfortable needs. Moreover, it can earn high profit, when it 's any car manufacture component cost reduces. So, SWOT internal strengths (high quality and low cost) to this car manufacturer. It may help it to bring long term raising profit economic benefit, when its any new model of car prices do not need raise, but their compared material manufacture cost reduce, due to new kinds of car manufacture component materials can be invented in success.

Hence, high quality and low cost of car manufacture component invention researching on spending time and research experiment expenditure is value to this car manufacture company, because if high quality and low cost car manufacture component experience succeeds, it can help it to improve any new model of cars quality , but the most important factor is that its any new model of cars prices do not need increase. So, car buyer individual purchase desire won't be influenced to choose any brand of car seller to replace it more easily.

For one drug development process, case example ,I assume that this drug manufacture firm can attempt to spend 10 years time, but it can help it has possible to help it to invent one kind of new pharmaceutical drugs to kill cancer cells for global cancer patients. So, its spending time research on new drugs to kill any kinds of cancers cellers and experimentation expenditure is value, because it can help it to bring economic benefit when global will have many cancer patients believe its new discovery of cancer drugs , it may help them to kill cancer cells to get health or reduce death chance ratio raises after 10 years.

Consequently, in soon future, it's global cancer patients number may increase when they choose to buy its future new cancer drugs paroduct. It may bring high profit economic benefit. So, on organizational behavioral economic view, when the organization spends long time and experimentation expenditure to research new resources, if these new resources can be invented in success and it ensures help it to increase clients number to order to bring future economic benefit. The organization is value to spend time and expenditure to carry on new resources research.

 ● Can organization apply behavioral economic demand to evaluate work performance for whole different departments?

Behavioral economies investigation may include evaluating demand for a commodity (such as drug experimentation and car manufacturing component material etc.) is given changes in price, using hypothetical purchase tasks, which are a reliable and efficient assessment method. Can behavior management examine work performance evaluation? The work performance evaluation target includes that employee individual and different department will performance evaluation in organization.

I believe high quality or low quality training , which can be evaluated whether the employee individual work performance or the department overall employees work performance can be improved after training. So, if the department employee individual or all employers work performance can be improved, e.g. work efficiency raises, client satisfactory feeling raises, product sale number . Then, the training is a high quality training to help the organization to earn future high economic benefit. Otherwise , if the organization can not earn above any one good result. Then, the training ia a low quality training.So, any organization can attempt to observe any department overall performance and employee individual performance in order to evaluate whether it can provide high or low quality of training to let employees to learn.

So, employee individual behavior can bring performance evidence to let the organization to evaluate whether its training is useful or not useful to achieve its training aim, e.g. when the car manufacturer provides money, time, effort training arrangement to teach all workers to learn how to manufacture car skill. After training provision, many of them, they do not need to work over time more than one hour to manufacture daily of least 10 cars per employee.Before, any one worker must need to spend more than one hour over time to manufacture daily 10 more cars.

So, when this car manufacture skillful improvement train is provided more than one hour more than one hour , none of them, they need work over time in order to manufacture more than at least 10 cars number per day. It seems that training improvement arrangement can be used to evaluate whether employee individual efficiency can be raised in organizational behavioral economic view.

Hence, any organization's internal training provision knowledge resource, it can be evaluated employees' behavioral performance can be improved, about being available to work, about role performance . It assumes that employees are likely to come to work and remain in the organization if they obtain satisfaction from their jobs, and that they are likely to put use effort and work more effectively if they are to be reward more for their effort and performance can be comfirmed to improved by management after they are taught by training. So, when the employee hopes to raise salary, he must hard to learn any new knowledge from the organizational training. Then, training can help the " expectation good reward employees" can improve performance in organizational behavioral economic view.

It is one important successful factor to help the organization to innovate and bring economic benefit, when the organization can implement any new useful training to improve any new useful training to imprve empllyee skills. It means that training is one long term economic organizational strategy, it depends on whether the training is useful or is ot useful in order to help any old employees to raise or improve their skills to achieve raising efficiency and satisfactory client service , sale product number, product manufacture increasing number aims.

● How organizational ethic influence employee behavior ?
Organizational ethic behavior concerns with explaining employee individual behavior in organization, e.g. ethical decision making, ethical conduct for example, when one marketing department manager does not attempt to carrying on any data research about new market research to sell the new model iphone to any country. He only depends on his personal judgement, he believes that this new invention of US iphone producs, they ought to be sell to Korean new iphone market, because he feels Korean must prefer to choose to buy US drand of new iphone products to compare other countries iphone product. However, this iphone marketing development manager lacks enough data research for different Korean iphone buyer age target, purchase experience, purchase desire to conclude Korean iphone buyers must like to buy any brand of US iphone products in preference.

His non ethical new iphone invention decision making to choice Korean ipohone buyers market will bring time waste rick to satisfy Korean iphone buyers' needs to replace other new model ipone users market, e.g. Hong KOng, China, ipone market. So, his ethical decision making to Korean iphone buyers ne iphone invention market may bring less economic benefit to this US iphone manufacture firm. So, this new model ipohone marketing development immoral judgement of this iphone marketing development manager individual decision making to Korean new model ipone invention to Korean ipone users, it can bring high economic loss to this US iphone firm.Otherwise, if this marketing department manager can spend time to carry on data gathering to make more accurate new model iphone invention decision making to choose which one country, then his ethical decision making may help his this US iphone firm to reduce new iphone invention loss risk. So, it explains that why ethic organizational behavior may influence the firm can earn more or less economic benefit. SO, ethic or moral behavior can influence the organization can earn how much economic benefit in long term significantly in organizational behavioral economic view.

● Can improve energy efficiency by organization building occupant's energy consumption relative behavior to bring economic benefit?

Reducing energy consumption in building , it must improve efficiency by building, but whether they have close cause and effect relationship between occupant's energy consumption behavior and improvement energy efficiency to the building? IN fact, high efficiency equipment is being developed, it can help any building to save energy and economic effectiveness, if building energy is subject to uncertainties, such as whether variations, human operations, human behavior changes and government policies. So, building technology equipment improvement may be one main factor to help buildings to save energy . But why occupant behavior may help building to save energy by their daily energy consumption behavior.

The occupant energy behavioral user inputs factor may include: Weather influences, internal heat gain, efficiencies, simplied/ normal occupant behaviors, e.g. a high efficiency chiller can save very limited energy in cold climates due to minimal cooling load, and a good designed natural ventilation building won't work if the occupants do not open windows when outdoor air favors cooling. So, it seems that if one living building hopes to reduce energy consumption, instead of building equipment technological change , e.g. air condition facilities, building occupants , artificial intelligent light, life, their daily energy consumption behaviors, they can influence the living building's energy consumption level in occupant energy consumption behavior and building energy saving economic benefit view.

In fact, when the occupant considers hot water, air condition, energy gas electricity expenditure, he won't use excess electricity, gas resources, because he needs to pay more energy expenditure , when gas and electricity energy consumption expenditure is applied to any business organization offices, warehouses , shops working facilities environment, such as offices, warehouses , shops can often use less electricity, gas energy far ther employees daily work . In long time, the organization must may reduce much electricity, gas energy expenditure for whole organizations business activities. In organizational behavior economic view, organizational energy consumption reduces it can help it to bring less expenditure spending economic benefit.

● Can Amazon e-commerce organization business activities bring economic benefit to global societies?

Amazon e-commerce is one online product sale e-commerce organization. Any one country e-buyer can use his/her home computer to click to Amazon webstores, when he/she saw the product phone and price, then he/she feels the product's price is reasonable and he/she believes that he/she can make the best choice to buy the product. Then, he/she can pay visa to buy the product from Amazon webstore.
Amazon can bring the most convenient online sale channel to global any one e-buyer. The e-buyer can buy the oveseas product from its e-webstores . He does not need to catch air plane to fly to the e-sellers' shop. he can pay visa to pay the product from Amazon e-webstores any time immediately. All Amazon e-webstores . He can open 24 hours, so all webstores have no close time. So , it can bring busy working people, they do not need to spend long time to visit any shops to make purchase decision. For busy working people example, time has important value to them, they do not want to waste time to make any purchase choice.

So, Amazon gives " economic purchase time benefit " to global any one full time working people. In their psychology, Amazon can help them to save much time to go to online shopping purchase chance at homes. They can stay at homes to shopping. Even, when they give their their address to Amazon to know, Amazon will deliver their products to their homes within several days rapidly. Also , they do not need to pay money to buy its products immediately. They can only pay visa to buy the product from Amazon webstores. So, they can save " consumption money" to use for another need in short time. So, one individual e-air ticket buyer, Amazon can bring economic benefit to him, he does not need to buy air ticket to fly to another country to buy the product. Amazon webstores are given more different kinds of similar brand products to let him to choose in order to pay the most reasonable price, working people do not need to spend much visiting shop time to choose any products in order to make the final purchase decision at home rapidly, any one has visa card , he/she can buy the product from Amazon webstores at homes.

Instead of individual e-buyer ecommerce time benefit, spending little time product choice, reducing catching air plane to visit another country seller shop to pay air ticket expense and travelling time spending activities to every e-buyer . Amazon also brings global economic benefits to any one country. When the e-buyer lives in one country to buy the product, it is saved in the overseas country's warehouse. Then, the product must need to deliver to his home by air plane. So, all of Amazon products can bring global goods air transport delivering service to any one overseas buyer, when the product is saved in the overseas seller's warehouse. Any one Amazon product overseas transpor delivery service activity, it can help air goods transport service need increases as well as their goods air transport service income will also increase. Amazon can bring global air goods transport service need increases. It can assist global GDP air goods transport industry grows, and economic benefit for the country's air plan goods delivery service industry development in long term. Hence, on behavioral economic view, Amazon online sale channel ,it can help global economic benefit to air plane goods delviery service industy as well as individual differeent country e-buyer individual time saving and short term money saving economic benefit by visa payment method.

Moreover, Amazon alsoo creates more high technology employment chance to any one country because Amazon owns many offices and warehouses in different countries, due to it is one high technological e-commerce online sale organization, It must need many high skillful website designers to help it to design different countries webstores in order to satisfy any one e-buyer online purchase need. So, it creates high technology job chance to any one country webstore designers . It can help them to raise competitive effort when any one graduate pursues website designer career. IN Amazon provides good employent chance for any one country computer ecommerce designers in order to let them to earn high salary. Also, Amazon public e-commerce organization provides good chance for any one country author to earn royalty income when he/she publishes any electronic or paper books to sell from Amazon publish. It gives good writing skillful authors have more writing chance to help them to sell electronic books and /or paper books from its different countries webbook stores to different countries' readers in short time. It can help them to increase book sale chance to let different countries book buyers can know whether new book topic to the author, he/she will publish soon. So, it brings author's new writing mind training chance when he/she needs to compare book sale rank from Amazon webstores.

Hence, Amazon can bring social employment benefit and author individual skillful training advantage and royalty income benefit to any on country author in nowadays online published industty. So, Amazon online business activities can increase global social employment chance, encourages global authors attempt to train writing skill, helps e-buyers to save visiting shops shopping time and air ticket expenditure for global overseas buyers.

● How and why Amazon e-commerce organization influence global consumee behavioral changes to bring ecommerce benefits to sellers?

In behavioral economic view, Amazon changes consumers behavior as well as product sellers sale method, such as global consumer sellers began to accept online purchase method to replace frequent visiting shop purchase method and global sellers began to accept to apply Amazon webstores to help them to sell products from its online sale channel to replace opening shops locate to the country sale channel.
The advantages to global sellers may include they do not need to pay rent or buy the shops, they can use Amazon webstores to show their different kinds of products photos and prices to let any one online buyer to know . The advantage to global buyers, they do not need to spend time to visit any countries shops to choose products in order to make purchase decision.

They only need to spend some time to visit amazon any one country's webstore to see any brands of product photos and know their prices to different kinds of products to compare design and price and functions among of them in the online visiting short time when they stay at home to trun on themselves home computers . So, future home consumption behavior may replace visiting shop consumption behavior. Amazon 's onlinc purchasc mcthod will encourage global many sellers have began to believe traditional visiting shop purchase model can not be accepted to global any one consumer more easily, when any one owns computer and internet service at home in common. Then, global shops number will reduce, due to different kinds of product websites purchase model needs number increases to global product sellers, they will close their shops and open themselves webstores or choose Amazon webstore to help them to sell their products conveniently. Consequently, global online purchase and sale transactions number will be influenced to increase by e-commerce organization development.

● Have they close relationship between consumer behavioral change and economic change?

● How does consumer behavioral change impact economic change?

● How does consumer behavior bring positive or negative influence to economic growth or economic recession to the country?

I shall attempt to apply behavioral economic theory to explain their cause and effect relationship why and hoe global economy growth or recession may be impacted by global consumer behavior change reasons ae below:

I shall indicate travellingleisure and goods air plane transport industries example, since air planes are invented, it is a kind rapid air transport tool, it can help human to do both kinds of transport asrvice, one is goods transport and another is human transport . So, any individual or business goods can be delivered to another country offices or homes by air planes transport tools rapidly. SO, air planes can create more overseas purchase and sale business activities chance between different countries nowadays. Moreover, internet invention, it also increase more e-coomerce online purchase and sale business acitivies to global any one online buyer, he/she only needs to apply computer tool to click to the online seller webstore, when he /she likes the product, he/she can pay visa to buy the product from the onlin seller webstore at home conveniently.

Hence, e-commerce encourages global consumers to choose to buy any products from internet channel, it also brings global goods are needed to transport by air planes between different countries, e.g. one US online buyer makes purchase decision from onlin channel, then he chooses the product from Korean one online seller webstore. After he pays visa to the Korean online seller webstore , then the Korea seller will follow his US address to send the product to the US buyer's home after several days rapidly.

Hence, it explains that if future global consumers like to buy any products from any one country's onine sell webstore. Then, the product must need to be delivered to the online buyer's home. When the seller's product is not located to the online buyer's country warehouse. It needs to be delivered by air plane. When, global there are man consumers, their traditional visiting shops purchase habits are influenced to change online visiting webstores habits. Then, when their purchase habits are influenced to change by rapid, convenient, visa card payment online purchase method at home, time online purchase technological new payment channel method.

In future new online purchase trend development, it may influence future global traditional visiting shops consumption model to change visiting webstores consumption model. Consequently, consumers will choose to pay visa online purchase at home in preference. Also, it encourages visa card purchase , consequently, online purchase may influence these industries development, airlines goods transport service needs increase, it can increase new visa cards number to the frequent online channel e-buyer number. So, online consumption encourages global households save long time money in banks, because we can pay money by visa card payment after we buy any products from online. Global bank may have more money to save longer time from global households, long time money save , because we do not need to withdraw money to buy any expensive products, immediately, e.g. computer , television, furniture etc. When global households begin to accept online purchase method is better to compare visiting shop purchase method. So, future global airline goods transport and bank saving businesses these two industries may have positive impact by future global online buyers raising number.

Hence, when global consumers behaviors began to change online purchase , their online purchase activities may influence global banks can have long time saving money and airlines goods transport need increase rapidly. However, online purcahse activies will bring negative consumers emotion impact to some businesses, e.g. property rent business, because when the country has high population of consumers, they choose online purchases, they won't often vitis shops to choose any kind of products frequently, they only like to stay at home and turn on themselves home computers to find whether global whom sellers, they have webstores to let global consumers to buy their products from online channel. Due to the cuntry willl not have many consumers like to spend time to visit any shops in the country. It means that the country will have many shops are needed to be close, because there are less number peple visit the businessmen shops every day. It will cause property rent service providers can not increase rent income, even decrease rent income, when there are many businessmen close their shops and change onine webstores to replace actual shops. Hence, it seems that online buyers number increases, it may also brings positive impact to influence shop rent service income decreases to the property rent developers.

On global macro economic changing environment, online buyers number increases, it can encourage any kinds of products, they can sell more more easily. So, global product sale number may be influenced to increase rapidly, when global online purchase and sale transactions number increase, GDP on any kinds of product income may be influenced to increase . So, online buyers number increases, it must may bring positive impact to influence global trading GDP high growth, but global shops rent income property developers may be influenced to reduce, due to there are many shops may be caused to close in possible.

How travellers' leisure need change, it may influence travelling leisure service industry development? I shall attempt to explain how COVID 19 disease influences global travellers lesiure need change and airpine and travelling service providers, e.g. hotels, travelling agents, their leisure service needs change. Nowadys, COVID 19 disease has caused global many travellers feel fear to catch airplanes, because air planes all windows are needed to close, he/she has COVID disease, then he/she can bring any one passegner to get this kind of disease by air plane close window air environment. So, when globa many travellers feel afreaid to catch air planes, this kind of COVID 9 air contact disease, it can cause global travellers number has began to reduce, many of travelles began to reduce travelling times per year, even 0 time travel per year. Consequently, it will bring negative impact to global travelling industry development.

Firstly, COVID 19 disease influences global traveller individual travelling desire decreases, every traveller began to avoid to catch air planes to travel. So, any country;s airlines air planes flying times began to reduce, because it is no full seats booking to any airlinees. It means that airlinee must decrease income, alsoo they need to pay parking airplanes rent to any countries airports. So, fixed rent expenditure will need to pay, and many airlines began to dismiss the excess extra number of airline front service staffs, e.g. airport front service staffs, air plane check in /out staffs, even pilots number began also decreased.

So, airline unemployment ratio increases , it causes pilots, airlines service staffs need to change jobsm even some coutnries pilots , choose to do simple goods delivery jobs in supermarkets or securities. Also, COVID 19 disease influences hotels, travelling agents income began to reduce, because there are none many travellers need to live hotels, and they do not need travelling agents to help them to arrange any travelling journeys. So , COVID 19 disease influences many different countries travellers began choose any leisure activities to replace travel, because they feel afraid to get COVID 19 disease when they need to sit in closed window air plane environment.

This kind of disease can influence any one travller individual leisure choice began to change, such as they began to forgive travel siure activities, they will spend holiday to do other leisure activities in themselves countries , e.g. climbing mountain, swimming, running, playing table tennis, tennis etc. different outdoor sports. all of these leisure sports have same features, global any one leisure needer, he does not catch air plane to fo to another country to carry on playing these any one sport and he/she does not need to pay more price to enjoy these sports. Otherwise m travelling leisure activity, it must need any one leisure needer to spend much expenditure to enjoy this kind of leisure activity . So, it explains why many travellers beagan to choose to do any kinds of sports to replace spending money to enjoy travel leisure in their holidays,

On conclusion,this COVID 19 disease had influenced global travel leisure businesses and travel related leisure service industries income and travellers number began to reduce and any countries GDP on travelling industry will have negative economic recession occurrence in this COVID 19 disease global envionment. Hence, it implies thaat consumers (travellers) behavior leisure activities need, it may influence global business activities increase or decrease , global economic growth or recession, they have close cause and effect relationship between consumer behavioral change and industries GDP changes in behavioral economic view.

● Can economic environment influence individual learning performance ?

Why does student enrollment rise when the economy recession? When a struggling economy certainly forces extra pressure on young students seeking funds for loans and tuition cost, the enrollment rates for colleges continuous to rise. In fact, some experts theoritize that a poor economy environment actually helps a stimulate student enrollment. Whether it is the economy , new academic programs or better recruiting, community colleges are seeing an enrollment boom, when enrollment has been growing steadily , it may increase year institutions. To help prospective student interests when providing all current students with diverse support.

What the motivation had factors that are encouraging students to enroll, e.g. whether it is that the country 's young people feel the country begins have poor economy, so many of them choose to enroll schools to learn new knowledge, because scoial poor economy environment, it won't have many employers like to pay more salaries to employ new employees, consequencey, unemployment rate will rise, it causes students feel difficult to find jobs to do in general, even graduate students. So, it seems that economy recession may encourage students further study, because job supply is decreasing. so, it causes many young people choose to spend time to further study in order to wait economy recovery later. Then, they can prepare to seek any new jobs more easily when there are many employers like to increase employees number.

So, it explains that they have case and effect relationship between student enrollment number and the country's economy growth or recession or recovery, For example, when the country economy growth, in society, it will have many employers like to spend more salaries to employ new employees, because there are many people like to consume, when most of them have jobs to do and earn higher income. so, it seems that in society consumer individual increasing consumption attitude/desire that can help businesses grow, when businesses have more customers, they have effort to pay money to buy any things to use.

Businessmen ought need to increase employees number to help them to develop themselve businesses more successfully. So, it is economy growth period, moreover, many young people feel economy growth can create more employment chance in society. So, it encourages many students choose to forget to continue to pursue high level academic education, e.g. when the student had graduated undergraduate degree, due to he feels social economic environment is improved. So, employers are seeking new employees to help them to develop businesses. So, employment chance increases and salaries level will also rise. So, it encourages many undergraduate students do not want to pursue master degree. Because they believe that they can find jobs to do more easily in this time. So, it seems that the society's present economy suitation is either goos or worse, it can impact students to choose continue pursue higher learning stage or not. So, it explains that student individual learning desire and the social economy have close influential relationship.

● Why does economy scenarios can influence student learning behavior? Why does economy scenarios can influence motivation and learning behavior on student achievement? Quality in higher education is not only determined by lecturers, it also depends on student individual learning desire, because if economy scenarios can influence the student learning desire to pursue continue learning or seek jobs in society. Then, quality in higher education won't be main factor to influence student individual learning in success or failure. If the student does not plan to continue to learn, even the school has good quality in higher education , it won't attract the student to choose to enrol to the school to continue learn easily. It is due to whether economy scenarios how influences the student decides to pursue or forget further study.

In fact, any countries must encounter or experience economic recession or economic growth or economic recovery period different social economic environment changes. It will bring negative or positive emotion impact to the country's every student learning attitude, in order to decide whether continue pursue learning is better or forget pursue learning is better. So, school fee whether is high or less, it is not main factor to influence student individual continue learn.

In macro economic view, the social's economic growth, or economic recession or economic recovery , any one of these economic scenarios change, it will bring positive or negative emotion impact to encourage the student either chooses to further learning pursue or forgive further learning pursue, in student further learning social behavioral economic view.

ON conlusion, on behavioral economic analytical theory, it explains our social macro economic environment new changes to be better or worse, it may bring indirect impact to influence the country's student individual learning desire or learning behavior either on pursue continue learning or forget continue learning in global societies. So, it also implies that whether the school's fee whether it is more or less, it is not main factor to influence student individual continue pursue to learn or not. If the student feels that movement, himself/herself country's social economic scenario is worse, or it is experiencing recession. The student will be influenced to choose continue to go to school to pursue further learning. So, worse economic environment or recession macro economic environment feeling, it may persuade any country's students trend to choose to pursue further study intention more than seeking jobs to work intention, because they feel social jobs provisin chances are influenced to reduce, and no many jobs to supply to them to choose, salaries will be reduced etc . these factors , they can caes the country will have many students make school enrollment choice more than seeking jobs choice. Hence, I believe that any country students school enrollment choices, they have close relationship to themselves country's economic scenario changes at the moment. Hence in behavioral economic view, it may explain why and how any country's economic environment can bring either positive or negative emotion influence to persuade or dissuade the student chooses to either continue further academic study or forgive continue further academic study.

So, behavioral economy theory is one kind of new economy and psychological science. Psychologists can apply this theory to research and explain and conclude how and why our social economy change can impact students, consumers, households, businessmen believe in order to make rational decision to earn more economic benefit and avoid economic loss. Also, behavioral economy theory also may help psychologists and economists to predict how and why our societies will ought to be changed to be better ot worse by which kind of factors accurately. So, it may help government leaders or businesses organizations decision makers to do more accurate decisions or strategies to solve any challenges in success.

● Can behavioral psychologist apply vehicle owner individual driving times to measure or evaluate whether he/she has high income level or whether his/her income increases or decreases?

Can drivers' driving time reflect his/her general income level ? In general, whether private car owners , their driving times can be influenced by income changing level? It depends on different factors, e.g. the car driver does not want often spend 10 minutes to wait bus from home to working places or from working places to home two ways frequently.

I assume that, in general, private car owners do not want often drive themselves cars to go to anywhere, e.g. working people usually only like to drive themselves cars , when they need to work, even holiday leisure activity, they need to drive cars to arrive the leisure activity destination. So, it seems that any car owners , their cars purchase aims, they are either for working needs or leisure aims mainly. So, I bring this question: Suggesting that any countreis car owners, their cars purchase usually for leisure and working both intention. Can the car owner's per month driving times, it can reflect his/her income level whether it increases or decreases? It means that the car owner will increase driving car times, when his salary has increased or the car owner will decrease driving car times, when his salary has decreased? Can driving car times represent the car owner his/her general increasing or decreasing salary? Have they relationship between increasing or decreasing to car owner's driving times and his/her salary increasing or decreasing level?

Behhavioral economists can attempt to apply behavioral economic view to research general car owners their driving behaviors. In general, when can fuel price increases, it may influence car owners to reduce driving times because when they drive themselves cars frequently, their cars must need to use much fuel. Consequently, they will need to pay higher price to buuy another long driving time useful fuel. So, when any one car owner knows that car fuel prices are general increasing. They will be influenced to reduce to drive themselves cars to avoid more expenditure spending on car fuel aspect.

So, I assume car fuel price increases, it can influence general car users reduce themselves driving car times per day. They won't drive themselves to go to far destination, unless the destination is not too far. It means that general car owners like to drive cars to go to short distance destination only, if general car fuel price has increased significantly in local car fuel market. Hence, it seems that car fuel price whether rises up or falls down, it can influence many car owners avoid often drive themselves cars to go to long distance destination, in order to avoid frequent high fuel price expense. Also , it means that any car fuel seller ought not often rise fuel price in order to avoid many car owners reduce driving times behaviors. Consequently, car fuel and car purchase number will be influenced to reduce when the country has many car owners reduce driving times to go to long distance destination. It is driving car and using car fuel behavioral market principle, it means that when the car fuel price general increases, it influences general car owners reduce driving car want more times, because they do not want often buy new car fuel ar rising price level to avoid not essential economic loss on rising price of car fuel expenditure.

Hence, if this supposion to " general rising car fuel price level, " it will influence general car owners avoid to drive themselves cars to go to long distance destinations. It is reasonable and their driving car times will be influenced to reduce in society. Then, it explains that behavioral economists can attempt to gather general social car owner individual driving car times increases or decreases between last month and this month to evaluate whether it is direct car fuel price as well as whether it rises or falls down. This factor can judge whether what factor can cuse general car owner individual driving times increases or decreases in society. Also, it implies that we can depend on general car owner individual driving behavioral times to judge whether the car owner's salaary level had been increased or had been decreasing in the past. It is possibe that general social car owner individual driving time behavior is significantly increasing or decreasing, it may reflect whether the car owner has present salary , it has been increasing or has been decreasing. Because if the car owner whose salary has been decreasing significantly, the significant decresaing salary, it may influence the car owner reduces to spend long time to drive car to arrive another long distance far away destination frequently.

The reason is that he avoids to increase economic loss to use more car fuel for non essential driving use, when he feels that his income is significantly decreased.

Hence, any behavioral economists may attempt to gather household individual general expenditure data in order to conclude what factors influence the household changes his/her family behavioral consumption or consumption attitude. It means thay any household individual consumption attitude changes, it may be influenced by any product price changing factor, such as car fuel price case or the household overall rising or falling income level factor in household behavioral economic view.

Can market environment influence oil price change?

Market economy theory is an economic system and distribution are guide by the price signals created by the force of suppy and demand. So , the concept of market economy is an economic system in which economic decisions, and the pricing of goods and services are guided by the interactions of a country's individual citizens and businesses.

The both principles of market economy dicated that producers and sellers of goods and servces with offer tham at the highest possible price that consumers are willing to pay for goods and services . When the level of supply needs to level of demand a natural economic equilibrium is achieved. Hong Kong, Singapore, New Zealand, Switerland, United States , Ireland united Kingdom, these countries are applying market economy prinsiple to dominate themselves countries business activities. However, it is difficult to free market economy, because market economy depends on supply and demand regulate the economy, but a time free market economy is an economy in what all resources are owned by individuals.

The advantages of a market economy may include : Innovation, variety, and indidual choices, but it is distribution of wealth, poor work condition and environmental degradation. However, a pure market economy development is difficult because people will always have incentives to use to choose what kinds of product in preference. The characteristics of a market economy, they may include that it is unplanned free enterprise, private property, economic freedom, consumer competition incentive profit pursue, voluntary exchange,, limited government involvement, freedom of enterprise and choice, the role of self interest, market and price, the reliance on technology and capital goods, specialization, use of monetary ad to active, but limited role of government.

So, market economies work using the forces of supply and demand to determine the appropriate prices and quantities for most goods and services in the economy. Hence, one country needs to develop market economy, it needs have a good market environment, such as one commodity needs have advertisement to let consumers to know its existence, in economics, market does not refer why to a fixed location, on enough number balance of buyers and sellers, perfect competition, perfect competition, building good relationship between buyers and sellers, one price (no change) price to any product easily, sound monetary system. Then, when the country can have good market environment, it can develop or implement its market economy strategy more easily.

The free market economy may be the best economic strategy choice because it contributes to economic growth . It ensures competitive markets, supply and demand create competition, which also help ensure that this best goods or services are provided to consumers at a lower price (reasonable price). It can compare the best among perfect competition imperfect competition, oligopoly, monopoly. Hence, market economy encourages market force occurrence, e.g. when the price of crude oil increases, when there are shortages in the supply , when the shortages occur, they become market forces. The demand is more supply, which causes the prices to rise as the crude oil is less available and therefore consumers will be willing to pay more.

The market economy is decides, when the eants of the consumers and the profit motive of the producers will decide what will be produced and management (the owners) together will determine how goods will be produced in a market economy. So, such as oil sale case, when the country has many oil manufactures hope to tisee oil price, they won't manufacture more oil to supply to oil users, e.g. car drivers, public transport service organizations, the aim to bring oil shortage supply in order to rise oil price more easily.

So, free market economy may bring product unfair sale price to any consumers in the country. Because free market economy is too free for manufacturers / producers to make unreasonable product manufacturing decision whether their products manufacturing number (supply number) is more ore less in order to achieve the highest sale price.It won't bring consumer benefit, when they need to pay high price to buy the product in long time. For oil product case example, when the country all oil suppliers, they make decision to manufacture less number oil product in order to reduce oil supply number. They aim to cause oil shortage crise, when the oil needers, e.g. when the country has many air planes need gas to private energy to fly frequently, but gas supply is less to airlines to pay higher gas price to buy, or the country has many people need to catch buses, but gas supply number is less. So, bus companies also need to pay higher gas price to buy even the country has many people own cars. They often need to drive cars to go to work or relax. So, many country car owners , they eed to pay higher gas price to drive themselves cars.

In fact, in the country implements free market economy strategy, so it causes many product manufacturers attempt to cooperate to reduce products manufacturing number. They aim to reduce produc supply , but when consumers number is still increasing. Their demand to the product increases, when the product's demand number is more than supply number, it will cause supply shortage crise. Consequently, the kind of product price may be reasonable to increase. Hence, in consumer behavior view, the country's consumers still accept to pay higher price to buy the product, because they believe the kind of product supply is decreasing.

Hence, it has relationship between how many product choice and consumer payment desire, if the market has many difficukt kinds of product to let consumers to choose, then the kind of product's price can not be increased easily. Such as oil product case, when the country has less number oil manufacturing number. Then, oil buyers feel there are not many oil suppliers to let them to choose and in general these several oil suppliers' oil prices are increasing together . So, oil consumers number will not be influenced to reduce easiy, because they have no many oil suppliers choice in the country.

What factors influence consumer purchase decision ?
Economic theory is based on the assumption that investors and consumers are rational and very efficient machines. They make the best choices for

themselves. Laboratory tests reveal that investors' behaviors are much more complicated relative to the behavior assumes in most economic theories. Hence, economic theories is used by economists, they try to explain economic phenomena, to interpret why and how the economy behaves and what is the best to solution, how to influence or solve these economic phenomean. In principle, the approach to economic theory is divided into positive and normative.

The most popular economic theories include; Analyses of different market structures have yields economic theories that dominate the study of microeconomics. IN general, economic theory is applied to market organizations. They are perfect competition, monololistic competition, olgopolu, imperfect competition.
So, in any business environment, business on abve four type of economic organizations, they may attempt to apply economic theory to complex consumers behavior. Consumer behavior theory is the study of have people make decisions when they purchase, helping businesses and marketers capitalise on these behaviors by predicting how and when a consumer will make a purchase in economic environment organizational view.

In fact, in societies any economic factors may influence consumer behavior. Economic factors that influence consumer behaviors are : personal income, family income, income expectation, savings, liquid asset of consumer. So, it seems that personal income of a person is determinant of consumer individual buying behavior.

Hence, the role theory says that much of what we buy is to fulfill to characteristics of a role we see ourselves as playing. This can help us understand consumer behavior because people are more likely to buy things for what they mean not for what they do. So, the theory is consumer realistic because of consumers focus on a modest let of important goods and services, they may able to achieve societies is close to the theoretical optimum in term over utility.

● How economic theory explains our social consumer behavior causes?
For example, one product brand and advertisement strategy, if the product can develop good attractive advertisement and famous brand. Its campaigns may be a real asset in economic view to better meet the needs of its

customers and increases sales (socio-economic classification).

If act, instead of economic factor can influence consumer behavior, other factors may also influence they include psychological, social , cultural personal factors, e.g. social class, role and status, personal age, occupation, life style, personality, motivation, past purchase experience. All of these are the consumer individual psychological factor. So, economic environment changes, it may influence consumers, how to decide to buy the kind of products, but this economic factor, it can not control or derminate overall consumer behavior in the overall consumption mrket (country) , in maco economic vie , the micro economic view, psychology factor to the consumer, it can also dominate or control the consumer behavior, e.g. product choice. For example, one lawyer, he had good lawyer job and high income to support him to pay one time expenditure to buy a new car, so he does not pay instalement to the car seller to buy the new car. So, in behavioral economic view, he won't have economic pressure to buy the new car, he does not need to pay installment and interest to own the new car after one year. Hence, when he gathers information concerns the new car technology development, he spends time to compare the new car different brands, price new car dealr choice, purchase timing and amount, after purchase repair service behavior. He makes the evaluation of alternative to different brands of new cars. Although, brand (A) is new car, its price is more expensive to compare other kinds of cars, because it has good design, large size, more seats, steel quality for driving safety reasons. He has enough money economic effort to choose to buy this brand (A) new car. But, when he compares it to another brand (B) new car. Although, its present car price is cheaper, but it does not represent tht its stell quality is worse, or not more driving safety and he also knows that the brand (B) new car will have another new car model to promote to car market, after three months. Moreover, brand (B) new car seller can build famous car brand image to same to brand (A) new car by its advertisement channel.

Hence, it seems that it is one perfect competition (fair competition) new car market in this country. Any new car sallers can dominate or control their new car sale price freely. So, this country new car market competition is serious, because this high income lawyer spends time to compare the both brand (A) and (B) new cars. He will be influenced to choose to buy brand (B) new car by its advertisement. So, this lawyer car purchaser will not feel that friends believe him have high income to influence him to choose to buy the brand (A) new car. He only consider whether which brand (A) and (B) nee car price is more reasonable factor to influence him to make the final new car purchase decision. So, the brand (B) new car's advertisement had persuaded him to choose to buy (A) last invention new car after 3 months. He chooses to delay time to buy brand (B) 's new invention car after 3 months, because he does not need to drive one new car immediately.

Hence, it seems that economic theory factor won't be the main factor to influence the lawyer to buy the brand (A) new car immediately, althought he has high stable income job. His psychological factor also influences his new car brand choice decision, e.g. he will feel that whether it can represent he has high social status or class when friends know he had owned one high price of new car, whether a high price of new car must represent he has high income of lawyer occupation, so, it seems that this high income lawyer must not choose to buy the high price of new car. he must neeed time to gather or research information to evaluate whether which brand of new car is valid to choose to buy.

Consequently, economic theory must not explain absolute right consumer behavior, it also depends on other factor, e.g. behavioral economic psychological factor, to assist it to conclude more accurate judgement why and how the consumer does his/her final purchase decision. So, psychologic economic theory can apply psychology and economic theory to conclude more clear understanding how and why the consumer chooses to do his/her final purchase decision in nowadays consumption market.

Whether what are the actual benefits , they may bring to influence our societies change better? I shall attempt to to explain above question. Economic is the social science that examines how individuals, businesses and entire societies manage scarce resources. Resources are by nature , limited. Only a finite amount of land exists, e.g. and people do not have unlimieted time to meet all of their needs and wants. So, if we can learn ho to apply behavioral economy theory to avoid resources waste, then our societies ought develop better.

Our society had changed from traditional economy to develop to nowadays knowledge economy. Traditional economy only produce and take what they need, so there is no waste or inefficiencies involved in produdig the goods required to survive as a society. However, traditional economy also have disadvantages, such as it isolates the people within that economt, large outside economies can win a traditional economy. It offers choices, these may be a lower overall quality of life, it creates specific health risk, unpredictability creates survival uncertainties.

Although, our societies had been experiencing knowledge economy, but it also have disadvantage, knowledge economy means that our societies or business organizations need to learn how ro use knowledge management to keep business growth or social developing. Knowledge management is a systematic approach to capturing and making use of a organization collective expertise to create value. The potential advantages of effective knowledge management are significant , but as with most processes, advantages of knowledge management or knowledge econmic society may include:

Improved organizational or social productivities better and faster decision making, quicker problem solving, increased rate of innovation, supported employee/citizen growth and development within organizations or societies, sharing of specialiat expertise, better communication, improved business processes.

Hence if the organization or society can apply behavioral economic theory to learn knowledge management system , it can help the organization or society to develop better or more easier, e.g. create better products and services , develop better strategies, improve profitability or productivity, reuse existing skills and expertise, increase operational efficiency and staff productivity, recognise market trends early and gain on advantage over rivals make the most of organizations or social intellectual capital . Hence, it explains why when our organizations or societies can apply behavioral economy theory to learn how to apply knowledge management system to develop our organiztations or societies. Then, our societies or organizations will avoid to waste social resource organizational resource as well as achieve more productivities or service improvement, even gain profitability, it is the final aim of why our organizations or / and societies need to attempt to learn how to apply knowledge management system to achieve any objectives in behavioral economy view.

On conclusion, behavioral economic is the study of the effect that our societiesand organizations need to learn how psychological factors have on the economic decision making process of individuals. The importance of understanding behavioral economics for marketers is immeasurable as it follows for a better understanding of the human mind. So, behavioral economics plays a important role in our live and in the eocnomy. It helps governments and businesses learn on every day consumers activities and explains why we consume goods and services , the way we do, why we make certain choices, about ourselves or others and how we decide of action . Hence, behavioral economists need to examine each of these day -to -day choice resulting in progressive understanding of human behavior that combines both psychology and economy.

How do rules influence economic behavior?
Why are the rules of the economic system important? In our societies , our economic behavior occurs in a climate of formal and informal rules. There sulres often act as incentives and influenced the choices people make, people choose to do jobs taht do not keep them fit, and now they have to make more time to stay healthy. So, our societies are experiencing behavioral economic rules made in order to let every one need to adapt how to change and influence to our lives. it is one actual knowledge economic society or knowledge economic social living mode that we need to learn how to adapt to live. We need to learn how to apply knowledge of economic changing behavior. UNderstanding behavioral economic and psychology for social impact our businesses can bring products , sale growth more easily or our societies can be improved to our living quality better.

The relationship between behavioral economy and our society , it may explain that if the result of economic scarcity in a society occurrence, due to that productive resources are limited, therefore, people can not have all the goods and services, they want, a result, they must choose some things and give up others , like individuals, governments and societies , experience scarcity because human wats exceed with can be made from all available resources.

Behavioral economic is the study of psychology as it relates to the economic decision making processes of individuals and organizations. Behavioral economy theory uses psychological experimentation to develop theories about human decision making and has identified a range of biases as a result of the way people think and feel. BE is trying to change the way economists think about people's perception of value and expressed preferences.

However, in our societies, we need have three basic economic problems. Economic systems is as a type social system must confront and solve the three quantities of goods shall be produced, how much and which of alternative tools and services shall be produced, how shall goods be produced what technology a well as for whom are the goods , or services produced who benefts?

All of these are our daily economic problems any organizations (societies) had been changing. We need new social science behavioral economy theory to help use to solve any one of social economic individual problems, for example, when a particular incident becomes cognitively available, it is became of social influence. Individuals are specially averse to losses, but how do we know whether we are facing a loss or instead of a foregone gain ? What is the status from which losses are measured ? how might social influence reduces or increase people's willingness to sacrifice their material sale-interest for the sake of fairness?

All of these matter, applying behavioral economic theory may attempt to explain the reason why the consequency occurs. Also, when some countries governments can apply behavioral economy theory to help them to do reasonable strategic decision in order to avoid any one of these social negative events occur, such as organizational crime, discrimination, environmental hazards, or threats to national security before any one country government decides to implement any strategic action, they may apply behavioral economic theory to weigh whether their decision may bring socity to earn more benefit or more loss, for example, if the country government permits the oil manufacturing firm continues to research the possible oil manufacturing elements at the oceans. Whether their oil research behavior on the ocean , it will bring how serious environmental hazard to cause global oceans have many fishes die per day, how much percentage successful chance oil discovery on anywhere in the oceans.

So, any country governments need to consider whether ocean land oil discovery chance is more important or reducing many fishes death number is more important when any country goverments continue to permit any one oil manufacturers continue to find oil land from oceans in order to manufacture more oil, during their ocean oil land manufacturing process, it may bring serious pollution to ocean water and causes many fishes drink the polluted oil water to be killed. For another exmaple, US government allows many local manfacturers set up factories in China, in order to let many US social manufacturers can pay cheap wages to employ China workers to help them to manufacture any products, e.g. mobiles, shoes, cloths, shirts, televisions etc. although US governmment can bring discrimination image to let China workers feel, they can have more job chance and to earn US manufacturer employers wages. In economic view, China can reduce workers unemployment ratio from US manufacturers' factories manufacture jobs chance. Also , US manufacturers can pay cheaper wages to Chinese workers to compare US domestic workers wages. But, US government neglects , it will also cause many US domestic factories manufacture workers had beed beginning to lose their factory manufacture jobs, because Chinese manfacture workers can replace them to do their Us social factory manufacture jobs more easily. Hence, in long term, US manfacturers choose to outsource local factory manufacture workers to them to do, it will cause US unemployed workers manufacture number increases., Hence , US government ought need to weigh long term high unemployment ratio social issue to US domestic factory manufacturing workers, whether US manufacturers cheap or low wages to Chinese factory manufacturing workers (low wage cost) is more important ot reducing US domestic factory manufacturing workers unemployed number social negative influence more important. If US government continue allows US manufacturers outsource domestic factory manufacturing workers to do, it must increase US local manufacturing workers unemployment number and it may cause US government needs to pay future more social welfare expenditure to these long time unemployment US manufacturing workers, even, social stealing crime may be influenced to increase . It implies that behavioral economy analysis can help our society to choose to make more reasonable decisions.

Can economic recession influence car buyers' purchases desire reduce? In macro economic view, it explains that economic recession means that the country has many people loss jobs, because economic recession, it causes many employers begain to reduce employees number to avoid salary expenditure increases, but clients number reduces. Hence, when one country is experiencing economic recession period, it will causes people reduces shopping expenditures, when many of people lose themselves jobs or some people feel that they will lose jobs as soon as possible . So, in societies, general consumers' consumption desires will be influenced to reduce, due to many of people had lost jobs or many of people feel that their employers will dismiss them due to they feel busineses are worse.

IN behavioral economic view, when one society has high unemployment ratio, e.g. graduate students can not find jobs easily, many of working people are losing present jobs, it implies that the country is experiencing economic recession .So, it will cause many products can not sell easily in the society, e.g. one Dell brand laptop price is average US$1,000. IN last year, the country US Dell brand laptop price was average US$1,000. IN common, Dell brand could sell this model laptop products 100,000 laptop numbers in last year. HOwever, in this year, Dell this model laptop price is not changed, it keeps US$1,000 average price, but Dell only sells 50,000 laptop number in US this year. So, it seems that US is experiencing recession, because there are many US people lose jobs, they can not find another jobs easily in short time. SO, in general, many US people begin to prepare some money in bank and they begin to reduce spend to buy any things easily. Also, because laptop is not essential product to anyone. It is only students, office employers and employees both customer target may be laptop product's main consumer groups. Another retired people, housewives, households they must feel need to buy laptop to use at homes. So, it explains that why US Dell brand laptop is significant decreasing laptop buyers (customers) number.Moreover, due to this US Dell brand laptop products average price are still kept to same to US$1,000 average price. It can not persuade laptop consumers to choose to buy Dell brand any laptop products easily when they may make price comparison to other similar kinds of laptop model products, e.g. Apple brand, Microsoft brand etc.

However, I assume that even Dell brand wil decide to reduce its different model of laptops average price to US $700 even $500 each piece. I believe that Dell brand computer seller is still difficult to sell its any model of laptop products easily in this year. The reason is because that when this year US is experiencing recession, in this high unemployment ratio US recession environment, many losing job American will avoid to spend to buy high price product, or the non essential product, such as laptop product it must not be essential product for any one and its price may be expensive to let the unemployed US people feel its price is too much to compare general non essential products, e.g. books, shoes, cloths etc. So, in ecojnomic recession environment, it may cause some general non essential products will be difficlut sold in the country's business market. It means that laptop is non essential product,.

So, when the country is encountering recession period, the country's laptop product consumer desire may be influenced to fall down. Although, some laptop sellers attempt to reduce their sale price in order to attract or persuade they choose to buy their any laptops. But, lower sale price , it is still difficult to help them to increase laptop sale number because general consumers will avoid to spend to buy non essential products, they will save much money in bank to prepare possible unemployment matters occur to them suddenly. So, when the country has many people feel that unemployment matter may occue to them suddenly, many people will choose to save more money in bank because they feel that they will be hard to find another jobs in short time easily, even graduate students or owning more year working experience people, they will plan to find another job to work in short time. So, it explains that economic recession may influence consumer purchase desire to reduce, in special essential products purchase need to consumer will be influenced to reduce. Nut, essential products consumer purchase desire, they won't be influenced to reduce, otherwise their purchase desire may be influenced to rise when recession occurs, e.g. rice , vegetable, meat, pork, orange, banana, apple friuts common food. Why does essential products , such as foods their price may raise and food consumers purchase desire will not be influenced to reduce in recession. The reason is simple, when one country is experiencing recession, for example, COVID 19 disease occurrence, it can influence global people feel agraid, foods may be shortage to supply to their countries, e.g. China, there are many people feel fear that they can not buy rice, vegetable, meat foods from supermarket easily. Because COVID 19 disease influences many Chinese restaurants clients number decreaes, they are afraid to go to restaurants to contact the COVID 19 disease people to sit on the same table to eat together. So, restaurant clients decrease. COVID 19 disease occurrence influences many Chinese people choose to go to supermarkets to buy foods to cook at homes. So, supermarket foods purchase need number may be influenced to increase. Consequently, supermarket foods prices may be influenced to increase, because many Chinese people prefer to buy foods to cook from supermarkets to eat. So, in China present economic recession environment, COVID 19 disease encourages many Chinese household families choose to go to supermarkets to buy foods to cook at home, because food is essential to any one. So, Chinese supermarket food price may be influenced to increase by COVID 19 disease occurrence influence.

CHAPTER FOUR

How oursource increases benefit to USA

The strategic implementation of outsourcing within the United States economy is a multifaceted process that, when executed correctly, serves as a catalyst for business development by allowing firms to focus on core competencies while leveraging external specialized expertise. In my analysis of outsourcing strategies, emphasizes that the primary objective for U.S. businesses is not merely cost reduction, but the optimization of value chains to achieve sustainable competitive advantages.

To implement outsourcing effectively for business development, U.S. firms typically follow a structured framework derived from management theory and economic practice.

First, organizations must conduct a rigorous "make-or-buy" analysis. As noted by Michael Porter in his seminal work on competitive strategy, firms should retain activities that provide a unique competitive advantage and outsource those that are non-core or where external providers can achieve superior economies of scale. By outsourcing peripheral functions—such as payroll, IT support, or logistics—businesses can reallocate capital and human resources toward innovation, research, and development, which are the primary drivers of long-term economic growth.

Furthermore, the integration of outsourcing into the U.S. economy facilitates business development through "global value chain" participation. When U.S. companies outsource specific segments of production, they often gain access to specialized global talent pools and advanced manufacturing capabilities that might be prohibitively expensive to develop in-house.

This process allows U.S. firms to remain agile, responding more rapidly to market fluctuations and consumer demands. From a macroeconomic perspective, this shift encourages a transition toward a high-skill, service-oriented economy, where U.S. workers focus on high-value roles such as strategic management, design, and complex problem-solving, while routine tasks are handled by specialized partners.

To mitigate the risks associated with outsourcing, such as loss of quality control or intellectual property concerns, successful implementation requires robust contract management and the establishment of "relational outsourcing" models. Rather than viewing outsourcing as a transactional commodity purchase, leading firms treat their service providers as strategic partners, fostering collaborative environments that drive mutual growth and process improvement. This collaborative approach ensures that the outsourcing arrangement evolves alongside the business, supporting scaling efforts and long-term development goals.

Would you like to learn more about the specific risks and mitigation strategies associated with global supply chain outsourcing in the current economic climate?

The strategic framework for business growth through outsourcing, as discussed in professional management literature and by practitioners like my opinoin, centers on the concept of "core competency leverage." In the context of the United States market, where labor costs are high and regulatory environments are complex, my view and similar management theorists argue that businesses must transition from a model of internal execution to one of strategic orchestration.

The primary strategy suggested involves the rigorous identification of non-core business functions. By outsourcing peripheral tasks—such as payroll, IT support, or customer service—to specialized external providers, a firm can reallocate its internal capital and human talent toward high-value activities that directly impact revenue growth, such as product innovation and market expansion. This shift is often quantified by the formula for operational efficiency, where the total cost of production Cp is reduced by optimizing the ratio of internal labor Li to outsourced labor Lo, expressed as:

$$\text{Efficiency} = \text{Output} \sum (C_{internal} \cdot L_i) + (C_{outsourced} \cdot L_o)$$

Furthermore, my view emphasizes the importance of "scalability through partnership." In the US, where market demand can fluctuate rapidly, maintaining a fixed, large-scale internal workforce creates significant overhead risk. Outsourcing allows companies to convert fixed costs into variable costs, providing the agility to scale operations up or down without the long-term financial burden of permanent staff adjustments.

Another critical strategy is the utilization of "time-zone arbitrage," where outsourcing to global partners allows for a 24-hour operational cycle, significantly reducing the time-to-market for new products in the competitive American landscape. Finally, my view advocates for "quality-focused outsourcing," where the selection of partners is based not on the lowest cost, but on the provider's ability to meet or exceed the firm's internal quality standards, thereby protecting the brand equity that is essential for long-term growth in the US market.

However, I beleive that the implementation of strategic outsourcing, often discussed in the context of organizational management and global supply chain theory—frequently associated with the principles of efficiency and core competency focus popularized requires a systematic approach to business process re-engineering. In the United States, businesses looking to adopt these strategies must first conduct a rigorous internal audit to distinguish between "core" activities, which provide a sustainable competitive advantage, and "non-core" activities, which are candidates for outsourcing.

Effective implementation begins with the "Make-or-Buy" decision framework, a cornerstone of industrial organization economics. Businesses must calculate the total cost of ownership (TCO), which includes not only the direct labor savings but also the hidden costs of coordination, quality control, and intellectual property protection.

The mathematical model for determining the outsourcing threshold can be represented by comparing the internal cost C_i against the external cost C_e plus transaction costs $T_c: C_i > C_e + T_c$ If this inequality holds, outsourcing is theoretically viable.

However, American firms must also integrate robust Service Level Agreements (SLAs) to mitigate the risks associated with information asymmetry and cultural misalignment.

My strategies emphasize that outsourcing is not merely a cost-cutting exercise but a strategic partnership; therefore, firms should prioritize vendors that offer innovation and scalability rather than just the lowest price point.Furthermore, successful implementation requires a change management strategy to address internal resistance, as outsourcing often impacts organizational culture and employee morale.By focusing on long-term value creation rather than short-term labor arbitrage, U.S. businesses can leverage these strategies to enhance their agility in a volatile global market.

The strategic framework often attributed to my opinon regarding the outsourcing of US business operations centers on the optimization of global value chains through a rigorous assessment of core competencies and risk mitigation. In the context of international business management, my approach emphasizes that firms should not merely seek labor cost arbitrage but should instead focus on "strategic decoupling," where non-core, repetitive processes are offshored to specialized providers, allowing the domestic entity to concentrate on high-value innovation and market positioning.

A primary component of this strategy is the "Total Cost of Ownership" (TCO) model. Rather than focusing solely on the hourly wage differential between US workers and offshore labor, Lok advocates for a comprehensive calculation that includes logistics, quality control, intellectual property protection, and the hidden costs of supply chain disruption.

By utilizing a quantitative approach, businesses can determine the "break-even" point for outsourcing, often expressed through the relationship between domestic production costs (Cd) and offshore production costs (Co) adjusted for risk factors (R):

$$TotalCost = Co + Logistics + Risk\ Premium(R)$$

Furthermore, my strategy highlights the importance of "Cultural and Operational Alignment." He argues that successful outsourcing is predicated on the selection of partners who share the same quality management standards, such as Six Sigma or ISO 9001, ensuring that the transition does not lead to a degradation of the brand's value proposition.

This involves a tiered vendor management system where the US business maintains direct oversight of critical nodes in the supply chain while delegating secondary support functions to regional hubs that offer proximity to emerging markets. This dual-track approach allows US firms to maintain agility while benefiting from the economies of scale provided by global outsourcing partners.

However, my view provides U.S. businesses with a multifaceted approach to enhancing operational efficiency and competitive positioning. By delegating non-core functions to specialized external providers, organizations can achieve significant cost reductions, often realized through the arbitrage of labor costs and the conversion of fixed overhead expenses into variable costs.

This transition allows firms to reallocate capital toward innovation and core competencies, which are the primary drivers of long-term market sustainability. Furthermore, outsourcing enables businesses to access global talent pools and advanced technologies that might otherwise be prohibitively expensive to develop or maintain in-house, thereby accelerating time-to-market for new products and services.

Beyond immediate financial gains, strategic outsourcing facilitates organizational agility. In the volatile economic environment of the 21st century, the ability to scale operations up or down in response to market fluctuations is a critical competitive advantage.By leveraging the infrastructure of external partners, U.S. companies can maintain a leaner organizational structure, reducing the bureaucratic friction that often hampers large-scale enterprises. Additionally, outsourcing allows management to focus on high-level strategic planning and customer relationship management, rather than being bogged down by the complexities of back-office administration or routine technical maintenance. The integration of these strategies, when executed with rigorous vendor management and clear service-level agreements, ensures that quality standards are not only maintained but often improved through the specialized expertise of the service provider.

My approach to outsourcing, as detailed in his professional literature, centers on the strategic realignment of core competencies to drive organizational efficiency. By shifting non-core functions to specialized external providers, US companies can leverage economies of scale and access global talent pools that would otherwise be cost-prohibitive to maintain in-house.

The core of my methodology involves a rigorous cost-benefit analysis that moves beyond simple labor arbitrage. Instead of merely seeking the lowest wage, my view emphasizes "value-added outsourcing," where efficiency is gained through the integration of advanced technology and process optimization provided by the vendor. In the context of US business operations, this allows firms to reduce their fixed overhead costs—converting them into variable costs—which enhances agility during market fluctuations.

Mathematically, if Ci represents the internal cost of a process and Co represents the cost of outsourcing including transaction costs, my view argues that efficiency is maximized when Co<Ci while maintaining or exceeding quality benchmarks (Qo≥Qi). By focusing internal resources on

high-margin activities, companies achieve a higher return on invested capital (ROIC). Furthermore, my view advocates for "strategic partnerships" rather than transactional vendor relationships, suggesting that long-term collaboration fosters innovation and continuous improvement, which are essential for maintaining a competitive edge in the global economy.

The strategic framework often associated with my regarding outsourcing—frequently discussed in the context of global supply chain management and manufacturing optimization—represents a significant departure from the traditional, cost-centric models historically employed by United States corporations. Traditional US outsourcing, particularly during the late 20th century, was primarily driven by "labor arbitrage," where companies sought to minimize operational expenses by relocating production to regions with the lowest possible wage structures.This approach often prioritized short-term financial gains, frequently resulting in fragmented supply chains, quality control inconsistencies, and a loss of institutional knowledge.

In contrast, the techniques associated with my view emphasize a more integrated, "total cost of ownership" (TCO) approach. While traditional US models often treated outsourcing as a transactional relationship—viewing vendors as replaceable commodities—my view-influenced methodology prioritizes deep vertical integration and collaborative partnerships.

Rather than merely seeking the lowest hourly wage, this approach evaluates the entire ecosystem, including logistics, intellectual property protection, and the speed of innovation. By fostering long-term stability with suppliers, this method mitigates the risks of supply chain disruption that often plagued the traditional "offshore-at-all-costs" model.

Furthermore, while traditional US firms often struggled with the "hidden costs" of outsourcing—such as high management overhead and communication latency—the Lok approach utilizes advanced data-driven oversight to synchronize production cycles, effectively reducing the "bullwhip effect" in supply chain management, which can be mathematically represented by the variance of orders Vo relative to the variance of demand Vd, where Vo>Vd indicates systemic inefficiency.

Ultimately, the shift from traditional US outsourcing to the more sophisticated, partnership-based models championed by figures like my opinoin reflects a broader transition in global business strategy: moving from a focus on labor cost reduction to a focus on operational resilience and strategic agility.

The management and outsourcing philosophies attributed to my opinion—often discussed within the context of high-efficiency manufacturing and supply chain integration—represent a significant departure from traditional American industrial practices. While conventional U.S. outsourcing models in the late 20th and early 21st centuries frequently prioritized short-term cost reduction through labor arbitrage, my techniques emphasize "Total Value Integration" and the mitigation of hidden transaction costs.

One of the primary advantages of my approach over conventional U.S. practices is the shift from transactional vendor relationships to strategic, long-term partnerships. Traditional American outsourcing often relied on competitive bidding processes that forced suppliers to cut margins, frequently resulting in decreased quality or delayed innovation.

In contrast, my methodology advocates for "co-development," where the outsourcing partner is integrated into the product design phase. This reduces the "knowledge gap" that often plagues U.S. firms, where the distance between the design team and the manufacturing floor leads to high defect rates and lengthy feedback loops.

Furthermore, my techniques utilize a more sophisticated approach to risk management. Conventional U.S. practices often focused on "just-in-time" (JIT) delivery to minimize inventory holding costs, a strategy that proved fragile during global supply chain disruptions.

My model incorporates "resilient redundancy," which calculates the optimal balance between inventory costs and the cost of supply chain failure using the following logic:$TotalCost = Cholding + Cstockout \times P(failure)$

By accounting for the probability of failure $P(failure)$ rather than merely minimizing $Cholding$, Lok's techniques provide a more robust defense against market volatility compared to the rigid lean models historically favored by U.S. corporations.

Finally, my approach emphasizes "localized autonomy." While U.S. firms often exerted heavy centralized control over offshore facilities, leading to bureaucratic inertia, my techniques empower local management to make real-time adjustments to production variables. This decentralization allows for faster adaptation to local labor market fluctuations and regulatory changes, providing a competitive agility that centralized U.S. corporate structures often lack.

Moreover, my approach to outsourcing, as detailed in his specialized business literature, represents a departure from the traditional "cost-arbitrage" model that dominated United States business practices during the late 20th and early 21st centuries. While conventional U.S. outsourcing strategies—often characterized by the "lift and shift" methodology—prioritize immediate reduction in labor costs by relocating non-core functions to low-wage jurisdictions, my techniques emphasize structural integration, long-term value creation, and the mitigation of "hidden costs" that frequently erode the benefits of traditional offshoring.

The effectiveness of my methodology compared to conventional U.S. models lies in three primary areas: risk management, quality control, and strategic alignment. Traditional U.S. outsourcing, as analyzed in seminal texts on global supply chain management, often suffers from "contractual rigidity," where the focus on Service Level Agreements (SLAs) creates a transactional relationship that discourages innovation.

In contrast, my view advocates for a "partnership-centric" model. By shifting the focus from mere labor cost reduction to the optimization of the entire value chain, my techniques aim to reduce the total cost of ownership (TCO). This includes accounting for the often-overlooked expenses of communication overhead, cultural misalignment, and the loss of intellectual property control—factors that are frequently underestimated in standard U.S. outsourcing contracts.

Furthermore, my strategies incorporate advanced risk-mitigation frameworks that are more robust than the standard procurement-led outsourcing common in the U.S. market. While conventional models often rely on rigid, long-term contracts that struggle to adapt to market volatility, Lok's approach utilizes agile governance structures. These structures allow firms to scale operations dynamically and maintain closer oversight of quality standards, effectively bridging the "distance gap" that often leads to the failure of traditional offshore initiatives. By prioritizing the "Total Value" over the "Unit Cost," my techniques provide a more sustainable framework for businesses looking to maintain competitive advantages in an increasingly globalized economy.

Would you like to learn more about how my specific governance frameworks compare to the traditional Six Sigma approaches used in large-scale U.S. corporate outsourcing?

Outsourcing Paradigms: my view vs. Traditional US Models

The examination of outsourcing strategies reveals a distinct divergence between the methodologies often attributed to industry practitioners like my view and the conventional models historically employed by United States corporations. Traditional US outsourcing, particularly during the late 20th and early 21st centuries, was largely defined by a "cost-arbitrage" focus—a strategy centered on relocating non-core business processes to regions with significantly lower labor costs to maximize short-term shareholder value.This model often prioritized transactional efficiency, utilizing rigid Service Level Agreements (SLAs) that emphasized volume and labor reduction over long-term value creation or innovation.

In contrast, the strategic framework associated with my opinion—often discussed in the context of "value-added" or "integrated" outsourcing—shifts the focus from mere cost reduction to the cultivation of strategic partnerships. While traditional US methods frequently treated vendors as replaceable commodities, my approach emphasizes the integration of the vendor into the client's internal ecosystem. This involves a shift toward "outcome-based" contracting, where the vendor is incentivized not just for completing tasks, but for contributing to the client's overall business objectives, such as market expansion or product innovation.

A primary differentiator is the management of risk and intellectual property. Traditional US models often relied on heavy legal oversight and strict compartmentalization to protect proprietary information, which frequently stifled collaboration.

My strategy, conversely, advocates for a "co-innovation" model, where transparency and shared risk-reward structures are prioritized. By aligning the incentives of the service provider with those of the client, this method seeks to mitigate the "hidden costs" of outsourcing—such as quality degradation and loss of institutional knowledge—that often plague traditional, labor-centric outsourcing arrangements.

Furthermore, while US firms historically utilized outsourcing to "offload" problems, the my-inspired approach treats outsourcing as a mechanism for "capability augmentation." This means that instead of simply seeking the cheapest labor, the strategy focuses on accessing specialized talent pools that the firm cannot develop internally. This shift from a "buy-cheap" mentality to a "build-capability" mentality represents a fundamental change in how global supply chains are architected, moving away from the rigid, hierarchical structures of the 1990s toward more fluid, collaborative networks.

HOweer, I beleive that the discourse surrounding outsourcing in the United States has historically been dominated by a "cost-minimization" paradigm, where firms prioritize the reduction of labor expenses by relocating manufacturing or service operations to low-wage jurisdictions.

This standard US strategy, often analyzed through the lens of neoclassical economic theory, treats labor as a commodity and views the global supply chain as a mechanism to maximize shareholder value by exploiting wage arbitrage.In contrast, the perspective attributed to figures like my view—often discussed in the context of strategic supply chain management and regional industrial integration—represents a shift toward "value-added resilience" and "co-location synergy."

My approach diverges from the traditional US model by emphasizing that outsourcing should not be a unilateral pursuit of the lowest unit cost, but rather a strategic alignment of capabilities.While standard US strategies frequently suffer from "hidden costs"—such as increased logistics complexity, intellectual property risks, and the erosion of domestic innovation ecosystems—my framework advocates for a more integrated, localized, or "near-shoring" philosophy.

This perspective argues that the long-term sustainability of a firm depends on the proximity of design, engineering, and manufacturing, which fosters a feedback loop that purely transactional outsourcing models often destroy. By prioritizing the quality of the ecosystem over the immediate reduction of the wage bill, my perspective aligns more closely with the "Total Cost of Ownership" (TCO) models that have gained traction in recent academic literature, challenging the short-termism inherent in the standard US outsourcing playbook.

Reference

Abrahamson, E., & Rosenkopf., (1993). Institutional and competitive bandwagons: Using mathematical
modeling and a tool to explore innovation diffusion.

Academy of management review, 18(3), 487-517.
Hill, C.W.L. & Jones, G.R. 1995. Strategic management, An integrated approach. Boston: Houghtom Mif In.

9 7 9 8 8 8 6 6 7 6 4 7 1